BFI FILM CLASSICS

. . . .

Rob White
SERIES EDITOR

Edward Buscombe, Colin MacCabe, David Meeker and Markku Salmi
SERIES CONSULTANTS

Launched in 1992, BFI Film Classics is a series of books that introduces, interprets and honours 360 landmark works of world cinema. The series includes a wide range of approaches and critical styles, reflecting the diverse ways we appreciate, analyse and enjoy great films.

Magnificently concentrated examples of flowing freeform critical poetry.
Uncut

A formidable body of work collectively generating some fascinating insights into the evolution of cinema.
Times Higher Education Supplement

The choice of authors is as judicious, eclectic and original as the choice of titles.
Positif

Estimable.
Boston Globe

We congratulate the BFI for responding to the need to restore an informed level of critical writing for the general cinephile.
Canadian Journal of Film Studies

Well written, impeccably researched and beautifully presented ... as a publishing venture, it is difficult to fault.
Film Ireland

FORTHCOMING IN 2002

. . . .

The Blue Angel
S. S. Prawer

I Know Where I'm Going!
Pam Cook

The Manchurian Candidate
Greil Marcus

To Be or Not to Be
Peter Barnes

Nargis, Muqri and Mehboob checking rushes on location

Mehboob with a village elder

MOTHER INDIA

मदर इण्डिया
. . . .

Gayatri Chatterjee

A BFI book published by Palgrave Macmillan

First published in 2002 by the
BRITISH FILM INSTITUTE
21 Stephen Street, London W1T 1LN

Reprinted 2008

The British Film Institute
promotes greater understanding
and appreciation of, and
access to, film and moving image
culture in the UK.

British Library Cataloguing-in-Publication Data
A catalogue record for this book is available from the British Library

ISBN 0–85170–917–6/978–0–85170–917–8

Series design by
Andrew Barron & Collis Clements Associates

Typeset in Fournier and Franklin Gothic by
D R Bungay Associates, Burghfield, Berks

Printed in China

CONTENTS

For Juni (Bijoyini Chatterjee) & Joy (Sandipan Chatterjee)

The village-woman Radha stands proud before the greedy usurer Sukhi-lala

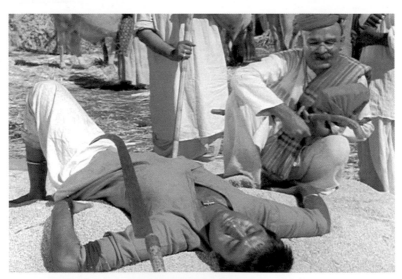

Rhada's son, Birju sprawls over the crop; the sickle will act as a weapon when need arises

ACKNOWLEDGMENTS

. . . .

It is possible, of course, to conceive even 'my time' as heroic, epic time, when it is seen as historically significant; one can distance it, look at it from afar … . But in so doing we ignore the presentness of the present and the pastness of the past …

M. Bakhtin in 'Epic and Novel'

This book would not have been possible without the generosity of Iqbāl and Shaukat Khān – sons of Mehboob Khan. When I began I was quite prepared to abandon the project, if I could not gather enough primary data to support and supplement analysis, theorisation and close analysis of shots and scenes. In a rare gesture (quite unprecedented in the Bombay film industry) they made available to me all the files and resources of the Mehboob studios. Shaukat Khan would say, 'Write what you want about the film and about our father, only see to it all your facts are correct.' I have felt happy and privileged to sit in the office of Mehboob Khan – amid trophies, framed letters and memorabilia. It was thrilling to open cupboards, and go through each file pertaining to *Mother India* page by page. The experience has changed me as a scholar of film studies in general and Indian cinema in particular. I thank all the office personnel of Mehboob Studios who helped take out material, make photocopies, scan photos, etc. I thank Nasreen Munni Kabir for introducing me to the Khans.

On some days, some shooting would be in progress. Assistant directors, cameramen, set directors, and sound-recordists, long associated with the industry and working still, deepened my understanding of how film practice in India is different today compared to 'those days, before everything changed'. Working in the environment of a film studio helped me greatly; those who populated this environment remain unnamed, but I thank them all.

A constant source of regret has been that I could only get to meet very few people who had been involved directly with *Mother India*. Those whom I was able to meet spoke with enthusiasm and without reserve. My sincere and warm thanks to Ali Razā, Naushād Āli, Sunil Dutt, M. A. Sheikh, Pāndurang N. Pātkar, Kāder R. Khan and V S. Thākur. At no point did they present falsely pleasant pictures of the past; each strove to be objective and subjective, critical and appreciative of the film and the circumstances of its making. Iqbal Khan at times would ask roguishly, 'So what do you think of this point?' and egg me on.

I am grateful to the following as each one amiably shared his or her particular expertise and helped in various ways: Abdul Āli, Anil Mehta, Ram Chattopadhyay, Monica Nerula (yes, I acknowledge all of you 'wildly'), Shuddhabrata Sengupta, Chris Pinney, Vivek Dhāreshwar, Āshish Rājādhyaksha, Trevis Smith, Ashok Rānade, M. F. Husain, G. U. Thité, Mādhavi Kolhatkar, Christian L. Novetzke, Uma Chakravarty, Shamita Gupta, Dilip Rajput, Jiténdra Kulkarni, Bijoyini Chatterjee and Sandipan Chatterjee. I thank all at the National Film Archive of India for their assistance in all my efforts.

I am particularly grateful to the following for their willingness to go through the manuscript at various stages, making important comments and corrections: Ron Inden, P K. Nair, Emmanuel Grimaud, Jibesh Bāgchi, Andrea Pinkney (it *is* all about collegiality), Ram Bāpat, Nasreen Kabir, Mini Śrinivāsan, Dipesh Chakravarty, Mādhava Prasād and Steven Lindquist. I have benefited at every stage of this book from the firm and friendly persuasion of my editor Rob White. Though arduous and nerve-racking, editing is a wondrous process; Rob White and Tom Cabot, also of the BFI, made it joyous too.

. . . .

I use diacritical signs for proper nouns only when introducing the word, in order to signal correct pronunciation to readers unfamiliar with Indian names. Afterwards, the practice is to carry on without them or with the way the name is normally spelt. Some spellings of names (like Krishna) are familiar to most readers – in such cases those spellings are maintained. All other Hindi and Sanskrit words, however, have been written with the diacritics, with the exception that common spellings of familiar words like *mahurat* have been retained.

'MOTHER INDIA'

The story of a film that receives great or even above-average success is the sum total of facts and figures, apocryphal and anecdotal stories, myths and legends. If the film was made some time ago, it is about memory – personal and collective. At times, it is necessary to be cautious. There is the claim, for instance, that ever since its first screening *Mother India* has been in uninterrupted distribution, always on the programme at some theatre somewhere in India. Thinking this to be an exaggeration based on the immense popularity of the film, I looked through correspondence between film distributors, theatre owners and the production company, along with bill-book counterfoils, theatre-hall reports and advertisements in daily papers – all preserved in the official files of Mehboob Productions in Bombay.[1] They confirm that ever since its first release in Bombay and Calcutta on 25 October 1957, the film indeed was in continuous circulation for over three decades – not only in India but all across the globe. However, this amazing history of film viewing and distribution did come to an end in the mid-1990s because of the boom in cable television and changing film-viewing tastes and habits.

Mother India, directed and produced by Mehboob Khan, was released in the Liberty theatre and four other theatres in Bombay. In

Radha sleeps at Shyamu's feet (they are a repeated motif in *Mother India*): from a deleted scene

Calcutta, it was released in the theatre chains Radha, Purna, Prachi and other suburban halls. Simultaneous release was considered for the Delhi circuit, but the première in Regal, Westend and Moti could only be arranged for 1 November 1957. By the end of November the film had penetrated every distribution zone in India.

The story actually begins some five years earlier. Mehboob's first colour film *Aan* (1952), a stupendous success in the domestic market, had also inaugurated international distribution on a scale unprecedented for an Indian film. Flushed with success, Mehboob launched immediate plans to make another film, to be in colour and titled *Mother India*. In October 1952, Mehboob's production company approached the Joint Chief Controller of Imports, for an import permit and sanction for raw stock sufficient for 180 prints. The maximum number of prints made for a film in those days was usually well below half that figure (usually around 60), and the JCC was not going to depart so sharply from the usual practice of releasing a limited amount of raw stock; and so protracted negotiations between the government and the production company began. The buying and selling of distribution rights, however, took off as soon as the project was announced in trade and film journals. Distributors already in business with Mehboob Productions and some new ones clamoured for the rights to Mehboob's new venture. The foreign distribution rights were sold from 1954 on. Cancellations and renewals of contracts mark the beginning of a film that was *famous*, even though merely at a stage of planning, governmental sanction yet to come – even before any clear decision had been taken regarding the story and cast. Apparently the process of *mythologising* had started at the conception of this film. Ivan Lassgallner, a distributor in London, had done business with Mehboob in 1952–4; he wrote on 8 July 1957, 'I hear you have completed your greatest film yet, *Mother Of India*' (he would later distribute *Mother India* in the European market). 'We will be privileged if we can distribute such a film as *Mother India*', an Indian distributor wrote in 1956.

Mythology is, indeed, one of the wellsprings of the film, as a look at the nomenclature in the film alone would confirm. References to gods and goddesses, representation of rituals and celebrations, songs and dances form the bulk of the two hours and forty minutes running time. Pre-existing motifs (tales, proverbs, aphorisms), familiar designs and iconography are worked into its narrative and visuals. As the saga of a peasant family, the eventful story encompasses a long time frame. In addition, the title *Mother India* is connected with various nationalist

Mehboob and wife, Sardar Akhtar with UK distributor Ivan Lassgallner (seated)

discourses and the history of India's struggle for freedom. The actors lend further lustre to the film's aura; some became stars and legends in their times, some went on to become prominent political figures. And yet the myths – those within the film and those surrounding it – cannot fully explain its phenomenal success. Films with mythological topics and overtones do not always enjoy critical and box-office popularity. Foreign audiences would not have understood all the specific references to Indian myths and traditional motifs, but nonetheless *Mother India* was successful internationally.

But to know the film well, it is necessary to uncover facts and histories: aspects of conception and production over a period of five years. The grand project, naturally, involved many people; most of the technicians and studio hands, scriptwriters and musicians worked full time in the studio and drew a salary. The actors – the stars and newcomers, those playing secondary roles and the extras – were contracted for a period of ten months, to be present fifteen days a month. They were, as some recall, members of a family, spending long hours and eating together – staying together while on location.[2]

Few people who had been associated with or witness to the film's production are around. But incoming and outgoing letters, notes and memos, bills, receipts and accounts are preserved (some are missing) within the covers of over a hundred files. Not everything in them is connected strictly with the film: there are records of community dinners on Fridays, banquets for dignitaries (often on the lawn, with liveried waiters), donations made to various organisations, film projects planned but abandoned, the director's attempts to improve film-making conditions in India. Together, they tell amazing stories, provide valuable information and help in the reconstruction of the film's history.

. . . .

Another starting-point in the story of *Mother India* is 1938, when Mehboob saw the Hollywood film *The Good Earth* (Sidney A. Franklin, 1937), based on a novel of the same title written by the American Nobel Prize-winner Pearl S. Buck. Mehboob planned to make a film on similar lines. But Bābubhāi Mehtā, a highly literate friend and source of story ideas, suggested another of Buck's novels, *The Mother* (1934), which chronicles the life of a Chinese woman – her life with her husband and her lone struggle when he abandons her. She surrenders briefly to the seductions of an official moneylender; scarred but eventually stronger she devotes her life to her land and sons. At the end, the mother is a mere spectator of changing times – seeing her youngest son get arrested for being involved in the communist movement. Fond of portraying strong women protagonists, Mehboob preferred this alternative and Mehta wrote a story that gave rise to *Aurat* (*The Woman*, 1940).

The heroine of Buck's novel is nameless, referred to only as 'the mother'. The heroine of *Aurat* is called 'Rādhā'. She is morally superior to the moneylender – indeed to everybody else. One of Radha's sons turns to a life of crime; unable to reform him, and for the good of her community, Radha shoots and kills her son. Indian audiences embraced this portrayal of extraordinary moral and emotional strength and advertisements and reviews hailed the portrayal of this 'quintessential Indian woman'. In 1952, Mehboob decided to base his new film on that earlier one, drawing upon that previous success. *Aurat* was being distributed internationally, as a result of the success of *Aan*, and the production company could be confident of foreign audiences too for the new film, the director's most ambitious project to date.

1938 was also the year when a Bombay film title, *Mother India* (India Cine Pictures), caught Mehboob's attention. Admittedly, Mehboob was jealous of its director Baba Gunjal and wanted to make his own *Mother India*. Normally film-makers tend not to repeat the title of a successful film but Gunjal's film had not been a great success. Besides, it was more than a decade since its release and no copyright protected the title now. The phrase 'Mother India' was filled with resonance, connected as it was with the national history of independence. India as a new nation-state was barely five years old at the time Mehboob's project was launched. So Mehboob was turning to or revisiting the past and was doing so in more ways than one. He planned to shoot extensively in and around the villages in which he and his parents were born and raised.

. . . .

Mehboob Ramzān Khān was born in the first decade of the twentieth century to a Muslim family from the region of Billimoria (formerly belonging to the princely State of Baroda) in Gujarat. His first years are not documented well, but there are several accounts by writers who knew Mehboob. His father Ramzan, the village blacksmith, was affectionately called *ghodé-nāl*-Khan, for his ability to fix horseshoes. Barely literate, but with some ability to read his mother tongue, Gujarati, Mehboob dreamt of other things for himself; he frequently visited the city of Bombay with a desire to be in films. A respected man of the village, Ismail-guard (a railway guard working between Baroda and Bombay) helped the boy in these escapades; but those first attempts bore no fruit. He was married to Fatimā (from a very poor family) and a son Āyub was born.

A family friend Parāgjī Desai later helped Mehboob to get work at the Imperial Film Company, owned by the legendary Ardeshir Irani, remembered today for *Ālam Ārā* (1931), India's first sound film.[3] Several versions of the story concur to suggest that Irani was impressed with the boy's strict adherence to religious duties (reciting the *namāz* at prescribed times of the day) and his horse-riding capabilities (Ramzan had been a cavalier in the Baroda State army). Irani gave Mehboob bit roles to play in his silent films, the first being one based on the Arabian Nights story,

Mehboob's first wife Fatima Khan with their first born Ayub Khan

A Mitchell camera in the
Mehboob Studios

Alibaba and The Forty Thieves (1927). Mehboob must have been in his
early twenties then. It is tempting to use a literary trope and say, it was as
if someone had opened the door to his destiny, calling out 'Open
Sesame'. But the fact is that the role was of no consequence; the camera
barely captured him. Years later, Mehboob would return as a director to
this same studio spot and shoot the first scene of his film *Alibaba* (1940).
The desire to return to the past runs through Mehboob's life and films.
During the initial days of struggle, Ismail-guard saw to it that Mehboob
slept undisturbed on the benches of the Grant Road railway station in
Bombay.[4] However, Mehboob soon made his mark as an actor. This part
of Mehboob Khan's life history is a 'rags to riches' story, a 'poor boy
makes it big in the city' story.

Talkies came to India in 1931. Mehboob was transferred to Sāgar
Movietone, another production house started by Ardeshir Irani.
Beginning with the lead in *The Romantic Hero* (1931), Mehboob made a
successful transition from silent films to talkies. However, he was
disappointed not to get the lead in *Ālam Ārā*. Similar professional
disappointments and his father's death (he was now the sole provider for
his wife and children) made him turn to direction. He joined up with
assistant cameraman Faredoon Irani and laboratory assistant Gangādhar
Narwekar. A Muslim, a Parsi and a Hindu were teaming up to do things
together – films were being made in those days about this kind of
cooperation. The studio heads decided to try him out and Mehboob
directed his first film, a historical drama, *Al Hilāl* (*The Judgment of
Allah*, 1935) – with the Katthak dancer Sitārā Dévī in the lead. She would
act in some of his later films, including *Mother India*.

An important part of Mehboob's city life was the chance to make the acquaintance of professional women singers and dancers (usually coming from a traditional courtesan background). *Village* for Mehboob was to mean, among other things, traditional marriage and community-based life. The *city* by contrast gave an individual the opportunity to satisfy romantic and sexual desires. Mehboob's debut film, however, was about wish-fulfilment of a different kind: the Roman emperor Caesar attacks a Muslim ruler (of a fictitious kingdom in the desert) and the local monarch resists successfully – the allegory, though clear, was ancient enough for the film to elude British censorship.

Mehboob came to be held as the 'Cecil B. DeMille of India' for his historical spectacles. Years later the Hollywood director would see a film on the Mogul emperor *Humāyun* (1945) and write to Mehboob, 'Motion Picture historians in this country generously credit me with having had something to do with fathering the film spectacle, and it is in this role that I wish to commend you heartily. Your compositions in *Humāyun* were fine, not merely in one instance, but in many scenes. One of the opening episodes – showing the column of horsemen moving away from the camera was a masterpiece of lighting and composition. I greatly admired many of the close-ups and found the score of native music quite intriguing.'[5]

Mehboob directed eight films under the banner of Sagar Movietone (this early work awaits proper appraisal). Sagar split up in 1940; some of its personnel joined General Films and formed National Studios, with financial assistance from the house of Tatas. Mehboob's first film under this banner, both a critical and box-office success, *Aurat*, is to be our constant point of reference. A year after its release, Mehboob married its lead actress Sardār Akhtar, a woman of many social graces. Mehboob had found his 'strong woman', a companion for activities at the studio and

Mehboob with Cecil B. DeMille in Hollywood

Mehboob with cameraman Faredoon Irani (and a guest)

travels abroad. Faredoon Irani, a strict disciplinarian, was attached to Fatima and the children (three sons and three daughters by now) and could not easily accept Mehboob taking on a second wife. Those who witnessed this exemplary friendship recall how the cameraman stopped speaking to his director for some time (it must be said, though, that this often happened), and only communicated during shooting via others. Mehboob was egotistical and possessed a volatile temper. At the same time, examples of his capacity to forge strong human relationships and draw love and respect are documented in office correspondences and embedded in the memories of those who knew him. And whatever his own personality traits, Mehboob viewed human relationships from many angles in his films and trod grounds other directors normally skirted around.

Most of Mehboob's films have been grouped according to genre, conventional since the Indian silent period: historical spectacle, musical, fantasy, action–adventure, melodrama (with each film drawing out a particular emotional situation, such as a love triangle) or social drama – often delineating the particular social life of Muslims in India. Occasionally, though, Mehboob made something entirely different like *Roti* (*Daily Bread*, 1942). This remarkable film stylistically follows German Expressionism (probably via Hollywood) and deals with the issue of money – a recurrent theme in Mehboob films. *Roti* created quite a stir, bringing further plaudits to cameraman Faredoon Irani.[6]

Mehboob Productions was established in 1943, an undertaking filled with risks, as World War II had made the world economy unstable and the future unpredictable. In India there was the added factor of growing agitation against British rule. On the other hand, there was plenty of fluid cash – 'black money' – from new ventures connected to the war effort. But there was no streamlined system of finance for cinema and Mehboob was forced to borrow heavily from various moneylenders. Thus after a long association with the medium, Mehboob entered whole-heartedly into the role of director–producer, in partnership with Faredoon Irani (later to be a director of the company) and Chimankānt Gandhi, an assistant since *The Judgment of Allah*. The office manage-ment of Mehboob Productions was undertaken by a group of dedicated personnel, headed by chief production executive V. J. Shah, whose absent presence accompanied me all through my research – every letter, if not signed by Mehboob, bears his signature.

Mehboob Productions' debut film *Najmā* (1943) was a successful Muslim Social (also a love triangle, with Sitara, Ashok Kumar and Veena). Two films that followed are relevant here, as *Mother India*'s heroine Nargis would play the lead in *Taqdīr* (*Destiny*, 1943) and *Humāyun*. *Anmol Ghaḍi* (*The Invaluable Watch*, 1946), a song-filled, brooding film, with undercurrents of humour, followed and ensured the director's popularity. The film's heroine, a poet, is in love with a poor man who in turn falls in love with her friend in a case of mistaken identity. With this film we begin to notice the director's propensity for depicting *weak heroes* a recurrent feature of Indian melodrama. But it is *Andāz* (1949) that really kick-started Mehboob's fame. The heroine (Nargis again) is independent-minded and given to the mores of rich feudal Hindu families that took to colonial ways. After the death of her father,

in keeping with his wishes, she marries a man of the same background, but entrusts the family business in Bombay to a nouveau-riche newcomer.[7] Unable to solve the problem of a 'second man' in her life, the heroine shoots this man, who had once saved her life, loves her now and takes care of her affairs. Within a decade, we see two of Mehboob's heroines taking up guns to kill men dear to them. In spite of it being a dark film, audiences liked *Andāz*, for its cinematic excellence and recognised it as an allegory of capitalism, rapid urbanisation and modernisation.

In a show of astute judgment Mehboob then made *Aan*, a colourful

Hollywood-style romance and extravaganza. But this alternation between dark and light films was not always successful. The next, *Amar* (1954), Mehboob's favourite, which has been critically acclaimed ever since, was based on the familiar allegory of *the city's rape of the village*, but it fared badly at the box office. In response to this disappointment, Mehboob launched three simultaneous projects, entrusting the direction of the first two, *Paisā Hi Paisā* and *Āwāz* respectively, to second assistant Mehrish and scriptwriter Ziā Sarhadi. *Mother India*, the third project, was delayed, while the first two were released in 1955–6. They proved to be even greater failures than *Amar*. So Mehboob was making *Mother India* after three successive failures.

In a situation like this a director–producer might make a small budget film – Mehboob chose the other option, the logic behind a big budget being *money begets money*. For *Mother India*, Mehboob sold film rights only to those who paid immediate advances upon signing a contract. For example, distribution in the city of Delhi was given to Indra Films for a sum of 400,000 rupees; both parties signed a meticulously drawn contract on 13 July 1955 – the producers received their advance. As the correspondence shows, the nature of their relationship and *modus operandi* was casual, and business mixed freely with personal goodwill. The very first letter, dated 8 August 1955, for

18   The westernised rich: Raj Kapoor and Nargis in Mehboob's *Andāz*

example, shows that at the distributor's request, Mehboob Productions handed over one hundred rupees to singer Latā Mangeshkar who had been raising money for charity. Beginning with *Andāz* she had been singing for Mehboob films and would sing for *Mother India* too. On 5 October, now at the behest of the production company, Indra Films made a donation of 300 rupees to a religious person in Delhi, 'for carrying out electricity work in his home'.[8] All this was officially accounted for. Vestiges of feudal pre-capitalist days reside in these files: human exchanges expressed through religious activities, oral promises carried out and noted at later dates, personal spending adjusted at times in the official account. Such social structures and ways still exist in many pockets of India, but the functioning of the Bombay film industry is, in general, vastly altered.

It is not clear when it was decided that one of the most important scenes in the film would be set during a flood and its aftermath. The north Indian state of Uttar Pradesh experienced devastating floods that year and a letter dated 13 September 1955 informs us that Indra Films had supplied Mehboob Productions with 'Cameflex (700 ft), Emo Exposed (200 ft) and some Gevacolor negative' for 'shooting the flood sequence'.[9] Faredoon Irani rushed to the flood-afflicted areas (Azamgarh district near Lucknow), travelling in rented military weapon carriers, since road and rail connections were broken. The first take of an Indian film, a particularly festive event called *mahurat*, is ritualistic and accompanied by religious ceremonies and parties. But *Mother India* began thus unceremoniously and under adverse conditions. Neither the script nor any decision about the cast was yet finalised.

After *Aan*, Mehboob wanted to go international and one way for this was to hire an actor from Hollywood. Sabu Dastogir, famous after *The Elephant Boy* (Robert Flaherty, 1935), flew over from Los Angeles. He was put up in the Ambassador Hotel and paid a monthly retainer of 5,000 rupees. A news item in *Film India* (run by Baburāo Patel who championed Mehboob's films, and would later change the title of the journal to *Mother India*) shows that there was a small *mahurat* ceremony for it, with the title changed to *This Land Is Mine*. Perhaps it was perceived that a film with an international star should be less region-specific. However, the government was still stalling over Mehboob's request for 180 print quota for *Mother India* and now there was a request involving further foreign exchange and also a work permit for Sabu. The Ministry of Foreign Affairs created further obstacle and delay at this point and asked for a copy of the script, anxious to check what the content of a film with such a title would be. By that time, though, Sabu had to leave – the previous title *Mother India* was reinstated.

The reason behind the call for the script was a certain literary work with the same title. American writer and social worker Catherine Mayo had written a sensationalist but poorly researched book *Mother India* in 1927. Mayo denigrated India for its lack of sanitation, child-marriage and other evils and suggested that British rule was a blessing for Indians, who were (as a race) incapable of ruling themselves. They might call their land 'Mother India', but they ill-treated her.[10] Government departments (the Ministry of Information and Broadcasting was also alerted) wanted to ensure Mehboob's film did not similarly belittle the nation. Mehboob's sons, Iqbal and Shaukat Khan do not think that, to start with, the film had anything to do with the book. But a script dispatched on 17 September 1955, along with a two-page letter, bears out how Mayo's book became part of the history of the making of *Mother India*: 'There has been considerable confusion and misunderstanding in regard to our film production "Mother India" and Mayo's book. Not only are the two incompatible but totally different and indeed opposite ... We have intentionally called our film "Mother India", as a challenge to this book, in an attempt to evict from the minds of the people the scurrilous work that is Miss Mayo's book.' Regrettably, the response from the government departments cannot be traced and the date when the sanction for foreign exchange and print quota finally arrived cannot be determined. But the project was approved. Accounts of obstacles in terms of finance, production and distribution lie buried within the files, reminders of problems Mehboob (and all film-makers and producers then) faced – counterpoints to the stories of success.

. . . .

Mehboob wanted his new film to be a spectacle, a potential box-office success; one way to ensure this was to make it in colour. He had already experimented successfully with colour in *Aan*, with Technicolor personnel Kay Harrison, George Gunn and Leslie Oliver (joint general managers: administration, business and sales, and plant and technical matters, respectively), suggesting some clever strategies to make it cheaply. *Aan* was shot in 16mm Kodachrome that followed a reversal process: a positive print was obtained straight away when shooting with this stock. A negative was made out of the positive, which then was blown up to 35mm and passed through Technicolor's three-colour separation (making three matrices) and dye transfer process.

Mehboob with (left to right)
Technicolor's Kay Harrison,
George Gunn and
Leslie Oliver

Mehboob wanted to make *Mother India* in 35mm. Of all available raw stock Gevacolor was the most preferred; it could now be processed in Bombay's Film Centre laboratory. A letter from A. J. Patel representing Gevart Products in India (22 October 1955) provides details of the new laboratory, processing techniques and estimates of the cost. But Gevacolor did not produce the saturation and definition of Technicolor. Of the few colour films made in the country till then, *Jhānsi Ki Rāni* (1953) was entirely in Technicolor, shot by the company's own camera crew. Mehboob would have no other but Irani shoot his films. But then after all the delay, Mehboob was desperate to start the film, so it was decided *Mother India* would be shot in Gevacolor and later processed in Technicolor. V. S. Thakur, working for Ramnord, Technicolor's agent in India (active even now in the Mehboob Studios), followed Mehboob's work closely. He recalls Mehboob's tremendous effort to bring the film to the release print stage as quickly as possible and dispatch it to the Technicolor office in London. Mehboob then proceeded to London for the final editing and colour correction, and Irani accompanied him for sound editing.[11]

Mehboob and Irani decided to shoot as much of the film as possible on location – 'A realistic spectacular drama', announced advertisements in *Film India*. Colour might add to the factor of seduction and spectacle: it can equally make a film realistic. Mehboob and Irani aimed for both – realism *and* visual splendour. It is interesting to note how many different locations were used for this film. *Mother India* begins with a card acknowledging the contribution of all the village chiefs. Of course, much of the film was shot in the studio. Most reviews were appreciative of the way the interior and exterior shots were blended: 'Interior-made shots are blended with the real. Color is good and technical aspect opulent,' wrote a reviewer in the American journal *Variety* (27 August 1958). Mehboob's studios were the best equipped in the country and the film team were perfectionists. A dedicated crew of painters, carpenters and set designers, electricians and light boys worked day and night to realise their vision. Contemporary cinematographer Anil Mehta remarks on the intricate tracks and pans, the detailed *mise en scène* patterns Irani conceived, even for brief shots – in the studios as well as on location.[12]

Mother India was shot mainly in synch sound, though dubbing was fast becoming the norm in the industry. The practice of recording dialogue and 'life sound' during shooting was known then as 'studio sound'. Only one microphone was used; the boom-man danced around cautiously, careful not to make any noise, taking the boom from actor to actor as each spoke. The boom-man was very important, as he adjusted the distance between actor and microphone, adding depth and perspective to sound design. M. A. Sheikh, assistant to sound designer/recordist Kaushik (another stickler for perfection), says that Mehboob thought dubbed films were 'soul-less'.

The dialogue of *Mother India* is a blend of vernacular Hindi and literary modes; the actors switch from one to the other, between lyrical, rhetorical and ordinary styles, with various degrees of ease. Occasionally some, particularly those making their debuts, had problems delivering their lines. Amusing tales accompany reports of Mehboob's perfectionism. Light-boy Kader Khan (later assistant to Irani) recalls how Mehboob went for scores of retakes, until he was satisfied. Repeated takes exhausted actors and crew. Once someone gathered courage and suggested the portion be dubbed. Mehboob would tend to decline, but dubbing *was* employed, as proven by the fact that actress Sheila Naik was contracted and paid for acting, singing and dubbing.

. . . .

Mother India begins with an outdoor sequence, but the first image of the film is a tightly held close-up of a face and not a classical panoramic establishing shot. The face belongs to an old woman, her skin the same colour as the earth she is sitting on, her face and hands as wrinkled and cracked as the dry mud. She picks up a fistful of earth and brings it reverentially to her forehead. A two-line chorus accompanies the image,

Quasi-documentary
images in the opening
sequence

'All our life Mother-Earth we will sing in your praise. And each time we
are born, we will be born into your lap.' The next shot reveals her in a
field under cultivation, tractors preparing the groundwork behind her.
And then, the images are only of such modern machinery and
instruments of development: cranes, concrete mixers, pylons, etc. A
second set of images is of a dam under construction by the side of a river.
After the two shots initiating the narrative and involving a character, the
film acquires a quasi-documentary quality reminiscent of documentaries
made under the aegis of the Films Division (a unit under the Ministry of
Information and Broadcasting). These images form the backdrop for the
opening credit sequence. The soundtrack is a mixture of instrumental
music and machine noise.

A high camera angle establishes a house, where the woman from
the first images lounges on a swing in a courtyard; children play nearby.
Men, in white clothes and caps associated with the ruling Congress party
of independent India, arrive in a jeep. One of them speaks loudly into her
ear: 'Mother, you know the water canal has come to the village. The
villagers want you to inaugurate it.' When the old woman declines with a
shake of her head, a villager approaches. 'You are our mother – *mother* to
the entire village! If you don't agree we will not start anything.' The
woman, bent with age, is brought to the site; someone approaches her
with a garland of roses, but she is reluctant to be so honoured. The son
insists and the garland is put on her – all without dialogue, pantomime-
like. The woman lifts the garland and sniffs deeply. The smell of flowers
initiates for her a recollection of the past; and a flashback begins: a long
dissolve transports the scene to her wedding day many years ago, when
her husband had put a similar garland around her.

If the initial sets of images suggest economics and politics, the wedding sequence images speak of culture and religion. If the initial images are realistic, these are bright – as made up as the bride. Through a series of dissolves, iconic tableau images in tight medium-length shots present the important stages of a Hindu wedding ceremony: the groom garlanding the bride; taking her palms in his; the couple taking their first seven steps together; going around a fire; her head being covered by a veil; the groom putting the vermilion *bindi* on her forehead and reddening her hair parting. A detail breaks in: a long dissolve of a tree on the figure of the bride, an overhead shot of scores of ox-carts idling around the tree in the cool of a grove. The last two shots of this sequence are dramatic, as there is an axis-jump – the cut coming after a series of dissolves adds to the effect.[13]

Two pairs of feet cross the threshold: the bride is leaving her *mother's house*. This leave-taking is a highly tragic-dramatic moment in

Mehboob's use of the axis-jump: the wedding sequence

the life of all families. Her parents look on – clearly village folks, chosen for that inserted shot. The traditional *Śahnāi* playing, accompanying the wedding sequence, gives way to a bride's leave-taking song. The *barāt* comprised of the groom's family take the bride away, the procession of carts rolls on. Extreme long shots of the carts traversing a large distance, in vast depth of field, are alternated with tight medium close-ups of the bride and the groom. The scene ends with a shot of a brilliant orange sunset with the distant, dark silhouettes of the carts. One image here is a citation of *Aurat*: the carts traverse a rivulet and a peasant is situated in extreme foreground, right of frame, accentuating the depth of field.

While explaining the situation to lyricist Shakeel Badāyuni and music director Naushad, Mehboob had exaggerated somewhat, asking them to imagine a poor girl all huddled up, 'holding on to her little steel trunk'. The feeling of pathos was to rivet the audience at the onset. Shamshād Begum, famous for her strong husky voice and expertise in folk music, begins, 'The beloved bride leaves for the house of her beloved. Her parents cry as if their entire life is wrenched away [*pīké ghar āj pyārī dulhaniyā calī*].' The beat evokes the uneven rhythm of ox-carts crossing undulating fields; the melody deepens the pathos of someone departing, while the cows return home at *godhūli* or dusk.

However, the mood shifts in the next stanza, as the song adopts the first person voice of the bride. 'My father and brother gave me all the happiness I needed. They presented me ornaments crafted out of stars and moons ... I travel, and with me travels the whole wide sky.' Asked to change from the previous mood and evoke the image of a strong woman, Naushad and Badayuni were reminded of a verse attributed to the seventeenth-century Sufi poet Amir Khusrow: 'My beloved, if I knew you would leave me, I would have set fire to my veil [*main ghunghat mein āg lagā déti*].' Significantly, a little later Irani does indeed light up the heroine's face from within her veil, providing the imagery of a woman with her veil as if on fire. The traditional mixing of a first and third person voice in the song is a good way to enter into or familiarise oneself with the structure and style of the film: its plurality, its various shifts of focus and interest, from character to character, topic to topic. Indian cameramen working within the idiom of popular cinema do not adhere to classical rationality when it comes to camera and lighting set-up. Instead they construct images in their own styles, and in keeping with the emphases of a director and a story. If the main themes and discourses within the film are multivalent, if the subjectivity, point of view and emotional content are plural, the camera work reflects that. Lighting then

Radha lit from within her veil

might not follow the logic of the single empirical light source; the editing might not be continuous and causal. *Mise en scène* is designed to express ideas and feelings.

The first-person voice continues, 'I possess no special quality. O my beloved, the shame and honour of the bangles (on my wrists) now rest on you.' *Kangan*, one of the most important narrative leitmotifs in *Mother India*, is a certain type of heavy bangle (or bracelet); here it is invested with dual meaning – marital and sexual happiness, material wealth and prosperity. The representation of the protagonist in *Aurat* was conventionally feminine: weak, soft and mannered. The heroine here was intended, by contrast, to be grander, larger than life. Actually, there is a pendulum-swing with the unfolding of this character – the heroine is strong as well as weak, ordinary as well as extraordinary. *Aurat* had ended with the death of the son at the hands of his mother; *Mother India* starts several years after that tragic incident in the life of its heroine. Advertisements in *Film India* announced, 'The Woman of *Aurat* has now grown old'. An actress was needed, who could convincingly act young and old, embody a wide range of emotions, attributes and mythical resonance.

There was no doubt in Mehboob's mind that Nargis was ideal for the role (initially some other names were considered too). Born Fatimā Rashidā in Calcutta, Nargis was groomed for stardom by her mother Jaddan-bāi, a woman of great talent and personality. Belonging to the courtesan tradition, Jaddan-bai was trained in literature, music and dance. She had acted in many films (she had played opposite Mehboob in *Nautchwāli*, 1934), had run a production company for some time and tried her hands at direction and music. Nargis had first appeared in *Talāsh-é-Haq* (1935) produced by Jaddan-bai (who had also scored the music, sung and played the lead in it). In her first lead role at the age of fourteen in Mehboob's *Taqdīr*, Nargis was paired with Motilāl, an actor several years her senior. Between 1943 and 1948 Nargis acted in eight films, often playing women much older than her actual age.

In 1949 she acted in two milestone films with Raj Kapoor as the hero – Mehboob's *Andāz* and *Barsāt*, produced and directed by Kapoor. She enjoyed working for a man of her own age (she had already acted in his debut film *Aag/Fire*, 1948) – rather than Jaddan-bai or Mehboob, both *father figures*. Going against the advice of her elders, she began acting in all Kapoor's films. Raj Kapoor and Nargis together embodied romantic love and sexuality in their performances in a manner unique for that period and it is widely thought that they were lovers off-screen as well. Less known has been Nargis's interest and participation in all aspects of film-making in Kapoor's productions.[14] But this star partnership was under stress at the time Nargis received the offer to act in *Mother India*. Perhaps she had begun to feel under-utilised and unappreciated for her overall contribution, which went far beyond acting successfully in the lead. Attracted by the challenge of the part, and realising its potential importance for her career, Nargis readily agreed to Mehboob's proposal.

Mehboob chose Nargis for the role of a traditional peasant woman, even though she excelled as a modern, independent-minded, sexually aware woman – the sexuality Nargis brought to the screen was not blatant or aggressive but touched with innocence as well as passion and a simple directness. The role of Radha required her to play a beautiful new bride, a young mother, a mature, middle-aged woman and finally an old woman, marked by physical and mental hardship. She was to play a *woman*, essentialised further as a *mother*. She was to internalise as well as to flaunt the sexuality that was her hallmark. This range of performance would surely render the audience's

Music director Naushad provided music for eight of Mehboob's films.

identification with Nargis multiple and varied. There is interesting contemporary evidence that audiences did identify with an actor playing different characters. When there was a delay in Mehboob's project, Nargis had signed up for a film *Miss India* by the humorist I. S. Johar. In it Nargis is a *modern* woman, who is also able to fulfil traditional duties and expectations. The film was released in March 1957. Nargis quotes a fan letter after both the films were released, 'Congratulations *Miss India* ... Sorry, I should say, *Mother India*!'[15] Audiences liked Nargis in very different roles; in this one film, they would see her in many incarnations.

. . . .

Colour plays an important role in the transformation of the actress, as her skin turns from the colour of mud to milk white. And again, colour acts as a means of codification. The old woman wore a dark red sari; now everything about her is bright red – the colour of love, passion and fresh, flowing blood. The bride's white, flawless skin is highlighted by red vermilion and *ālta* (a dye extracted from lac). Her hands, feet and forehead are emblazoned with the dye – a *swastika* design is drawn on her palms.[16] Bejewelled and bedecked, the new bride, identified with Lakshmi, the goddess of wealth and good fortune, steps into her new home.

The women of the family and village surround the groom: he must distribute gifts, only then will they allow him to enter the bridal chamber. The main narrative has begun. Following longstanding cinematic convention, static iconic images give way to narrative ones. The space is opened up; the camera becomes mobile, choreographed with characters' movement. Carefully worked out *mise en scène* and editing strategies (shot/counter-shots, point-of-view shots, eyeline matching, etc.) come into play. The groom is dazzled by his wife's beauty; her eyes are modestly closed in response to his ardent gaze. Drama and action follow after the slow lyricism of the earlier sequences. The man whispers dramatically the name of his bride, 'Radha!' – the first word spoken since the flashback began. Unable to withstand his prolonged gaze (or perhaps following prior instructions from elders) Radha falls at the feet of her husband in a gesture of unconditional surrender.

In the course of fifteen minutes, the woman is identified with three Hindu goddesses, connected with different religious traditions and discourses, signifying for the devotee various boons and benefits:

1) *Dhartī-māta* or Mother Earth: productivity and stability.
2) Lakshmi: beauty, wealth and prosperity.
3) Radha: consort of Krishna and the personification of love.

Radha is a heroine or *nāyikā* – romantic and proud, capable of great passion as well as anger. The recourse to mythology in *Mother India* is no cliché but carefully and elaborately worked into the film. The groom's name Shyāmu is a rural version of Shyām, the dark one – another name for Kŗśna (Krishna).

At the break of dawn, Shyamu's mother, Sundar-chachi (or aunt to the whole village) and other women have gathered in the courtyard around baskets of cotton seeds, plucking cotton and discussing the wedding. One comments that the new bride is as beautiful as Lakshmi. Another remarks, 'what use is mere beauty [*rūpa*]: she needs to have the right qualities and virtues [*guṇa*] as well?' All goddesses are beautiful, possess special qualities: but, *rūpa* and *guṇa* are especially associated with Lakshmi. The bride has brought a big dowry, but in order to meet the wedding expenses her husband's family house has already been mortgaged to the village moneylender. When questioned, Sundar-chachi wants to save face and denies the suggestion as pure gossip. But once she's back inside the house, she mutters to herself, 'How else could I celebrate the wedding?' She hopes the arrival of the bride will prove fortunate and the house will be freed. She muses, 'Radha does seem lucky!'

Sated after the wedding night, the groom sleeps; awake before him, but not daring to leave the room, the bride massages his feet. Shocked at what she has just overheard her mother-in-law say, Radha removes her ornaments one by one. All this while, Radha had been going through the

The actress Jiloo-Maa as Sundar-chachi in *Mother India*: she had previously played the same role in *Aurat*

motions as tradition and society dictated, now she acts on her own volition. A bride is not allowed to take off her ornaments, the visible tokens of marriage.[17] An ornamented bride ensures her husband's fortunes; the logic being *wealth begets wealth*. Radha's next move is to take upon herself all household chores. In a sharp departure from the stereotypical portrayal of a mother-in-law, Sundar-chachi is appreciative of Radha and says, 'Why do you do everything, let me also do something.' She pretends to be angry with the couple for their open show of love. 'What will people say?' and murmurs gleefully, 'How can I scold them! Shyamu's father behaved no differently.' Actress Jiloo-Maa, an old associate of Mehboob (they had acted together), had played the same role in *Aurat*. She is clearly at ease with the character, as well as being comfortable with her director.

Shyamu wants to engage in amorous play with Radha, but she labours from dawn late into night. He grumbles, 'Why have you removed your ornaments so soon? If not of yourself, think of me! I haven't yet seen you [as a bride] properly.' And as Shyamu tries to put them back on her, Radha utters her first words in the film, 'Sell them!' The selling of gold and silver is another taboo, conducted only under duress. Like her mythical counterpart, Radha is *mānīni*, a proudly resolute woman. Shyamu insists on putting the jewels on her, for he loves to see her in them. Radha now becomes *mugdhā nāyikā*, the coy heroine. 'I will take them off every day, so that you can put them on me every day, with your own hands.' Radha takes Shyamu his lunch in the fields and asks politely whether she has put enough salt in the food. Shyamu says, 'You have so much salt in you, whatever you touch becomes salted,' and pretends to lick the salt off her hand.[18] Family friends Kamalā and Shambhu eavesdrop, hiding inside haystacks. How often films allude back to and underline the element of voyeurism they have set into motion!

Radha and Krishna were never married. Devotees have lamented the eternal separation or *viraha* of their favourite divinities, seeing it as a reflection of their own separation from the God they worship. Sorrow and yearning have also been seen as necessary conditions for creativity. Centuries of musicians, painters, writers and poets have drawn inspiration from their stories. But a question becomes inevitable: why is this couple, depicting conjugal love, named after the divine but unhappy lovers? *Mother India* is not unique in borrowing myths but what is of interest here is the way the film mimics the mythical process. The appropriation and growth of epical/mythical material in *Mother India* is gradual and accumulative, spread over the entire narrative and visual surface. And as this happens some mythical elements are mutated, some are changed, turned upside down – subverted even. The mythological material and the contemporary narrative are in dialogue but also, at times, in conflict.

. . . .

Mehboob was strongly attached to his village and its community, going back whenever possible. He regularly met farmers and the religious heads of these villages, supported educational, religious and other endeavours (even today Fatima Khan divides her time between Billimoria and Bombay). Both *Aurat* and *Mother India* are filled with the immediacy of that familiarity, with sentiments remembered and nurtured. Mehboob was also a charismatic city-man, influential, commanding tremendous respect in the industry; he loved the city of Bombay, too. The director was not naïve and had the courage to fill his films with his own ambivalences. His films, till now, had shown he could be equally critical and appreciative of both the village and the city. But now another tendency was coming into play as *Aurat* was transformed into *Mother India*. He was now to engage with something bigger and grander: the idea of the nation (and all the sentiments that go along with it) – something one can only imagine or partially grasp. Such an effort is bound to stretch the limits of any imagination.

The first page of the publicity booklet for *Mother India* includes a quotation from the German Orientalist Max Muller, of which the first sentence is, 'If I were to look over the whole world to find out the country most richly endowed with all the wealth, power, and beauty that nature can bestow – I should point to India.' Max Muller had never visited India. Nations, one's own or someone else's, are often imagined. Creating an image of the nation means imagining homologised forms, human figures personifying abstract qualities: beauty and goodness, wealth and power, poverty and exploitation, community spirit or spiritual malaise. All were to be represented in *Mother India* through the many characters, much as in folk theatre.

The old script of *Aurat*, written by the crazy genius Vajāhat Mirzā, was to be reworked now. Mehboob liked keeping up with the contemporary literary scene and retained several scriptwriters and freelancers, who prepared for him synopses of books (fiction and non-fiction). Young Ali Razā, employed for four years prior to this film, was asked to work on the screenplay; but initially Razā was hesitant to make changes to the work of Mirza. Meetings were held to discuss the old script and formulate the new one; apart from Mehboob, Mirza and Raza, there would be Āgha Jāni Kashmiri, Ziā Sarhadi, Akhtar Mirzā (all scriptwriters), Naushad, assistant director Chimankānt Desai and many others. It was like a gathering of village elders: all opinions were discussed and silent disapprovals acknowledged, but Mehboob made the final decisions.

Mirza and Raza wrote the dialogues for *Mother India* from scratch and received joint credit for doing so. But, Mirza was upset that his name was associated with a mere novice and so protested to Mehboob and Raza. In a letter to Mehboob, dated 18 October 1957, Raza requested the removal of his name from the credits. 'Mirza has wanted to hear the voice of my *conscience*', he wrote, attaching with it Mirza's letter to him and his reply – both in the Urdu original and an English translation. Raza paid respects to his senior colleague and had written, 'I sincerely feel that my contribution towards the dialogue is not worth my name along with yours.' The film was about to be released – Mehboob made no changes in the credits.

. . . .

Unlike the divine couple, Radha and Shyamu cannot spend time in loveplay; they work in the fields shoulder to shoulder – as equals. Radha in *Aurat* was shown involved only in household chores, perpetually washing vessels and clothes. Like most women in rural India, Radha in *Mother India* works outdoors and as hard as the men. Within the house she cooks and feeds her husband, brings him his tobacco. The day ends with her massaging his feet till he falls asleep – this form of *sevā* or service, which younger members of the family render to the elders, is a repeated motif. Typically, there is no fixed place for Radha to sleep. The ordinariness and privation of Radha's life are carefully integrated, as counterpoints to the association with divinity.

There are other differences between the two films: in *Aurat* the heroine was glamorous while her husband was with her. Radha here is slowly stripped of her adornments, except for the essential signs of marriage: vermilion *bindi* on her forehead and *mangal-sūtra*, a black string necklace (with a pair of small round pendants). The reason behind this gradual impoverishment is one person, Sukhi-lālā (the moneylender alluded to earlier in the context of the mortgage of the house but now seen in person). Mehboob's village is neither a Utopia nor 'abode-of-peace' as painted by an Orientalist pen. The evil here is personified in Sukhi-lala the village grocer or *baniyā*, as the suffix *lālā* denotes – he is widely addressed as Lala. He is also the *sāhukār* – usurer or moneylender.

A page from the publicity brochure

A show card: publicity material distributed in cinema halls

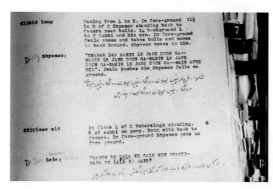

A page from the script: Ali Raza's handwritten notes in Urdu

Radha pays respect to the mother-earth

Radha as a Laksmi-bride

Bullock-carts carry Radha away from her natal home

Villagers celebrate a
bountiful harvest

Radha and Shyamu clear
a fallow land

Sukhi-lala manipulates the
village elders in his favour

Radha feeds her family

Radha looks for Shyamu
everywhere

Ramu toils while Birju
loafs

After the flood, Radha and sons toil under a painted sky

Radha and her community: a brilliant example of dissolve, so popular with Mehboob and Irani

The flooded acres: Radha stops the exodus

Lakshmi must be witness to Radha's disgrace

Radha challenges the mother-goddess to take on the role of motherhood

The wheel of life

Champa and Ramu
dancing at dusk

Rupa racing in a cart

Chandra imparts her
insight into usury to Birju

Radha enters the fire to save her son

Radha takes the life of her son

Radha's palm and the floodgate of blood-water

Lala exercises his control and power over the village by harassing the women. He stops Radha and Kamala (wife of Shyamu's friend Shambhu) on their way to fetch water and in the guise of speaking to Kamala tries to get acquainted with Radha. His words are sexual innuendos, dressed up as expressions of concern; he advises Kamala to be careful, lest she slips and falls on the 'slippery ground'; he pretends to be worried her 'mud pot' will be broken. Kamala, apparently the only one in the village who can stand up to him, hisses out, 'Women's steps do not falter as men's do. And thanks to you, no household can afford copper pots.' The man is insistent, 'Here I am prepared to give you a golden pot, but who listens to poor me.' Kanhaiyālāl Chaturvedi had already played Sukhi-lala in *Aurat;* he received 10,001 rupees for acting in *Mother India*: the only actor, it seems, to have got this additional one rupee – a mark of respect.

In order to strengthen the realist thread of the film Nargis and actor Raaj Kumar (as Shyamu) had familiarised themselves with farming practices: manoeuvring the plough, reaping and sowing, cotton-picking, etc. They varied their acting mode to suit the film's varied levels of realism and stylisation. Any number of elements break into the realism attempted at the beginning of the film, as is most noticeable in the song and dance sequences. Radha and Shyamu sing and dance in celebration of romantic love and youth, but they do so while they work. The dancers performing alongside the two couples were not extras from the Bombay film industry, but members of village dance troupes; this makes such a difference, adding to this song picturisation a naturalness or freshness rare in most films of that time. Instead of actually dancing, they strike poses with sickles and shovels. It is as if these Indian farmers have adopted Soviet-style cooperative farming, but are singing and dancing in traditional Indian fashion (some forms of cooperative farming were indigenous to western and southern India).

Some images, though in colour and with heavily made-up actors, have reminded several critics, among them Ashish Rajadhyaksha, of films by celebrated Russian film-maker Dovzhenko. A *Cahiers du Cinéma* critic commented that *Mother India*'s outdoor shots 'could be seen as referring to American (King Vidor) or Soviet (Dovzhenko) cinema'. It is very probable Mehboob and Irani had seen Vidor's *Our Daily Bread* (1934), released in Bombay theatres in 1939. How much of Soviet cinema they were familiar with is difficult to determine, but they certainly knew the works of Pudovkin (who had visited India in 1952). Many of the images here resemble posters by Soviet Constructivist painters; those must have been familiar to the film team as many (Mirza included) belonged to the Progressive Writers' Association of the left. Naturalist portraits of happy farmers, sickles in their hands, smiling from behind ripening crops were familiar, too – from the covers of the popular journal *Soviet Land*.

Shyamu's friend in *Aurat* is the romantic and handsome 'Bansi', meaning 'the flute' – the principal symbol of Krishna as a pastoral hero. After Shyamu's departure, the hero is present through his friend, their names being metonymically connected. Shyamu's friend in *Mother India* is Shambhu, short in physical stature and funny-faced – more of a jester (*vidūṣak*) than a hero's special friend (*sakhā*). Popular comedian Muqri normally played the good-natured fool and had acted in many Mehboob films and was exceptionally close to him. In one shot during the song, Shambhu picks up a large piece of bone, the femur of some animal. This strange, out-of-place image compels us to look once again at the factor of nomenclature. Shambhu is another name for the Hindu deity of dance and destruction, Shiva, who has many attributes: occasionally he is playful, occasionally a withdrawn ascetic, residing in crematoriums, his body covered with ash and bone. Surprisingly, advertisements in small-town vernacular newspapers at times bore photos of these secondary characters Shambhu and Kamala. Śiva-Śambhu is an aspect of this god that rural people take as their own – villagers dance annually *at his wedding*. However, this character is of little narrative importance to this film. The village community finds greater representation in the earlier film, while the epic-style *Mother India* is far more hero-oriented.

At this point, we might say the hero is the couple, Radha–Shyamu. But this traditional-modern hero-couple's passions are not epic-size, and their song is filled with ambivalence. 'Our hearts are crazed with love; the

Friends Kamala and Shambhu

rain-clouds have gathered. O you mad ones, love while you can, for life is short [*matwālā jīyā*].' The fertility of the land arouses sexuality and the men sing to their women, 'Give me a sign that is you [meaning progeny].' Kamala is childless and her husband wants her to bear children. Kamala playfully rejects Shambhu's sexual overtures and hands him a dried marrow shaped like the womb. (Kamala's childless status was much discussed in *Aurat*, but not so here.) The end of the song is accompanied by the announcement of Radha's pregnancy. A traditional farmer sees woman and earth as synonymous: both promise fertility (the agrarian term is borrowed by the natural sciences). Shyamu had asked Radha for a gift of four sons; he is crazed with joy at the birth of the first. He rushes to distribute good news and the crop, the yield of his land, among the villagers.

Sukhi-lala intervenes and claims from Shyamu three-quarters of the yield as his share. Sundar-chachi reminds him that he is entitled only to one-quarter. It now becomes clear that she was tricked into putting her thumbprint on a different contract. Lala has defrauded and lied to her. She refers to a tradition of trust in *verbal* promises; but her protestation is of no use. Shyamu is enraged, but helpless as the villagers are united in their cowardice. The village patriarchs – real villagers in cameo roles – support Lala, since they are and will always be indebted to him in many ways. They are unanimous on another account, 'The police must never enter this village.' They do not want to lose their traditional hold over legal and civil matters – besides, they do not trust colonial law enforcement.

The cycle of twelve months with its six seasons and the episodic nature of a farmer's life are highlighted in the next song – borrowed from the boatmen-song tradition of eastern India. The farmers lament, 'Millet is being cut, while our lives are shortened. The work is arduous, our life empty, our mad hearts filled with worries [*juhuriyā kattī jāyé ré*].' Song sequences in popular studio films often signal the passage of time or an ellipsis in the narrative. In the course of this song, two more sons are born to Radha. The song ends with the couple looking up at the sky, as if trying to divine the weather and their destiny. In a match-cut, the moneylender is shown looking up too, but he is looking at the balance-hands, while weighing his share of cotton. In the same shot Sukhi-lala looks down; the camera tilts down to find the couple squatting on the floor, stricken and despairing.

The family sleeps at the end of this long, event-filled sequence. The camera tracks in gently and comes to rest on their second son, Birju, sleeping with his head resting on his father's legs. The camera movement indicates the narrative importance of the character.

. . . .

Two gods separated chronologically by a *yuga* (an aeon, a full cycle of civilisation) are brought together in this story. The eldest son is called Ramu: the affectionate form of Rām, the principal protagonist of one of the two great Indian epics – *The Rāmāyan*. The second is Birju, another name for Krishna, a key dramatic persona of the other epic – *The Mahābhārat*. Birju means one who hails from Braj, the village where Krishna spent his childhood. Radha's two boys are polar opposites – the youngest two (one of whom is not yet born) are never named. The divine Ram is considered one-of-supreme-good-character and just-towards-his-subjects. So the eldest son, Ramu, is good and obedient, loving towards his younger brothers. Birju, by contrast, is mischievous and disobedient, as young Krishna often is. Popular Bombay films are known for the depiction of morally polarised brothers (and at times sisters), who personify good and evil. *Mother India* has been considered the origin of this motif, inaugurating a whole genre, as it were.[19]

The representation of little Birju borrows from stories of the child Krishna (who is worshipped in his own right). Birju is extremely lovable, though precocious and mischievous. But, his misdemeanours stem from his knowledge of Sukhi-lala's hand in the misery of his family. Curious about the oppressor, Birju visits Lala's opulent house and catches his daughter Rupā eating gram and molasses – *canā-guḍ*. The children are caught in striking frontal images: a big ornamental Burmese-style wooden cashbox fills the frame, with the children on either side. Birju

Rupa, Birju and a cashbox

snatches away Rupa's bowl; Lala is enraged, but Sundar-chachi arrives just then, asking for a loan of millet for her starving family. Lala suggests she pawns the family utensils when she refuses to part with Radha's jewels. Trading, lending money and the pawnbroking of land and property are related activities, perpetually at odds with the community values of the village (as David Hardiman has discussed). Chachi knows no other way of life and there is a certain intimacy grown out of *village-connection* between her and Lala. She does not feel inhibited begging on Birju's behalf for some of the *canā-gud* Rupa is eating.

Birju screams in rage, reluctant to let go of the bronze and copper vessels, holding on to his favourite plate. Radha tells him he must concede or else his father, brothers and grandmother will starve. The boy weeps, 'Would *you* starve too, mother?' and relents. Radha's love for her eldest son is deep and constant; but her relationship with Birju is special and particularly highlighted in the film. Not only is Radha partial to Birju, Mehboob was as well – as is clear from the amount of narrative and visual attention Birju receives. Sajid, a son of poor, estranged parents from a Bombay slum, was found for this role. His father signed the contract on his behalf (since Sajid was a minor) for 750 rupees. Sajid as Birju proved very popular with audiences and critics; and he captured Mehboob's heart. So taken up was the director by the little boy's acting ability and street-smart ways that he and Sardar Akhtar practically adopted him.[20]

Birju as an active narrative agent is first seen sitting on a heap of grains, supervising payments being made to farmhands, acting the grown-up. Lala wants the employers' grain-share to be taken out of Shyamu's quarter and not initially from the total yield. 'Have you worked on the plough that you want the grain?' asks Birju, echoing sentiments that one deserves only what one has toiled for. Birju's resentment of Lala is deep – atavistic even. The strength of his feelings wins audiences over to him. Similarly, they would be quick to locate the villain of the piece in the person of the usurer, whose oppression is both part of collective memory and contemporary experience. A pre-colonial, pre-capitalist practice, extant even during the British rule, Lala's form of usury was very much a reality for Indian farmers even at the time of the film.

Radha takes Birju to the village school (which Ramu already attends) and pleads with the master, 'Please teach him arithmetic so he understands Sukhi-lala's accounts.' The teacher replies, 'Even the British government is unable to do so!' Literacy is an important but subtle theme in the film; but, in this introductory sequence, it is associated with corporal punishment. Birju will not meekly submit to the master's favourite form of punishment and hits him with his catapult. The image of Birju bound to a post – his grandmother has punished him for that misdeed – is a familiar one from mythology. According to legends, the boy Krishna was punished for stealing his parents' butter and cream and breaking village women's water pots.[21] Secretly approving and amused, Radha unties her son and feeds him. Her sense of duty is eclipsed by her love; but the grounds have been prepared for the final dramatic moment, when the call of duty will override everything else.

....

Radha wants to cultivate some fallow land the family owns. The moneylender can have no claim to its produce, she thinks. As they try and clear the area of rocks and boulders, one of the two oxen dies. Lala comes home to take away the other: this will pay off some of their debts, he says. Shyamu, enraged, goes for his throat, but lets go at the insistence of his mother and wife. The seed of rebellion against traditional usury is there in Radha's husband, but will ripen later, in the person of her son, Birju. Radha opens her dowry box and suggests another ox be bought in exchange for her remaining ornaments.

Shyamu thus fails to remove an obstacle and eradicate a menace, Sukhi-lala. While clearing the barren land, Shyamu tries to uproot a big boulder, by tying it with a rope – Radha and the ox pull from the other end. Shyamu urges, '*sabbās* Radha, keep it up.' But the boulder rolls back, trapping his two arms – they have to be amputated. If we see this film as Radha's story, then it is *her* misfortune her husband can no longer work on the land. Radha is the central figure of the narrative: the narration is initiated by *her* recollection and memory. But the film until now has not created any clear viewpoint: both husband and wife have been equally important. If we refrain from privileging the woman character just yet, we appreciate that the film's first major disaster falls on Shyamu.

Sukhi-lala takes away the remaining ox one day in lieu of payment of interest due, after calling Shyamu a coward who lives off his wife. Shyamu has become increasingly aware and ashamed of his disability and this is the last straw. That night, while the rest of the household is fast asleep, Shyamu leaves home for ever. But before leaving, he wipes the red vermilion mark from Radha's forehead – a sign that from now on she should consider him dead. It is worth noting the way Shyamu is different in *Aurat* and modelled after the husband in Buck's novel. He is weak, restless and increasingly abusive towards his children and wife. Shyamu in *Aurat* did not leave because of accident and disability; he wanted to

Ramu, Radha and
Sukhi-lala in *Aurat*

escape the infernal cycle of work, debt and family responsibility. Birju's negativity, as is clearly indicated there, is the result of his father's neglect and abuse. Shyamu, in his later incarnation in *Mother India*, is hard-working, responsible and caring; he leaves only because he believes himself a burden to his family.

Perhaps it is time to justify this frequent reference to the former film. Every time we do so our understanding of *Mother India* gains an extra dimension. The observation of these changes and choices – what to retain, what to change and the nature of the changes – reveals the intentions of the director, scriptwriters and others. Author's intentionality is a contentious issue, of course, and often questioned as a valid critical tool. However, as in this case, if it is possible to know how much or what sort of deliberations went into the making of a film, the knowledge can only add to a study of the film. The point is not to judge to what extent *Mother India* is a remake of *Aurat*, though it is interesting to note that the former owners of National Studios (which had long since gone into liquidation) had gone to court with a case of copyright violation. On 17 July 1957, Mehboob's lawyers wrote to the liquidator, representing National: 'He [Mehboob] got the script work done somewhere in 1938 by his friend and colleague Mr. Babubhai Mehta. Mehboob allowed your company to avail itself of the said story with its scenario only for the first production of the same ... The Company never obtained any copyright in respect of the said story either from Mr. Mehboob nor from anyone else.' The case did not proceed: the plaintiffs were satisfied with an out-of-court settlement.

. . . .

The fact that Shyamu cannot assert himself and somehow defeat Lala can be taken to suggest a moral weakness. He does not think of staying on to provide his sons with a father and Radha with a husband. As if to underline this emotional-moral failure in him, the very next sequence shows the arrival of the fourth son. The dyad, the ideal union of man and wife, is split asunder, and the male half rendered useless and redundant. The other half must now become increasingly stronger, able to support four infants, help them continue with their lives and more. Questions have been raised as to why the film-makers decided to have Shyamu disappear rather than die.[22] Death would have meant a permanent split of the couple – total destruction of the dyad. Widowhood would have rendered (in the particular Indian context) Radha ineffectual – sapped of life forces. But instead of that diminution, if she is now to acquire divine status or become a super-mother, she must retain all of her sexual and sacral powers. Having him leave means the marriage is not dissolved and Radha remains associated with sexuality and productivity. Shyamu might have wiped off her *bindi*, but Radha continues to wear it – for her Shyamu is always absent, but ever-present. The narrative persona meets squarely the one she is named after. Radha is to spend her life in eternal separation from her husband.

Radha looks for her husband in temples (temporary shelter for those who abandon or are abandoned) and sings a song immortalised in the voice of Lata Mangeshkar, 'I look for my beloved in every city, every threshold [*nagarī nagarī dwāré dwāré*].' Radha sees her husband everywhere; the song uses flashbacks to the time she was with Shyamu. At dramatically crucial moments, as here, the film makes further use of flashbacks – within the main narrative that is itself a flashback. Temporality in epic narratives is spiral-like. Radha is *continuity* personified, stable and patient like Mother Earth. Such a protagonist must live long and experience several births and deaths, several rotations of joy and sorrow. Sundar-chachi dies; Radha sells her last pair of bangles to perform the last rites and feed all the village *brāhmans*. A strong denouncement of brahmanical practice (in the context of an impoverished village) is contained in a single but powerful shot, accompanied by a conversation in voice-over: Birju protests, 'You're feeding them sweets and we don't even get bread!' We hear Radha add, 'Yes, feed sweets to the dead [to propitiate ancestors] and starve those who are alive.'

Radha now becomes the head of the family and the issue of motherhood grows in importance. Mehboob wanted motherhood to be significant in a number of ways, mostly staying within traditional ideas, at times going beyond them. The synopsis sent for governmental approval opens with the declaration that the film is about the 'eternal theme of Indian woman' and closes with a comment about a mother 'round whom revolves everything that is sacred and glorious in our culture, tradition and civilization'. One could wonder speculatively whether and how different the film might have been had there been less governmental intervention. Motherhood is a contentious issue, often meagrely discussed (as E. Ann Kaplan has pointed out) – unfortunately, discussions that this film could generate lie beyond the scope of this book. Images of motherhood can represent, in a patriarchal society, strong ideals of community and stability. But it is also motherhood that highlights the labours demanded of women in such a society. In *Mother India* both aspects of maternity come into play. Some images are undeniably positive and appealing, for example the ones with Nargis and her infant third son (Master Alec) sitting happily on her lap, smiling throughout. The subjective pleasure of a mother when with her child is rarely shown in films (if so, usually for some narrative or ideological end). So both sets of images – one in which the representation of motherhood is exploitative and serves patriarchy by showing a mother suffer, the other in which female subjectivity is celebrated in the figure of a woman capable of working, loving and striving to live – are present in *Mother India*. Images like that of the baby eating and drinking on his mother's lap or Nargis picking cotton while carrying him tied to her back are not merely ornamental; work is a theme and not a mere backdrop against which the story unfolds.

Typically, the idea of the nation as mother was exploited in India both for colonial ends and anti-imperial ones. In literature, music and painting, the idea was an important tool for nationalism and the freedom movement. *Bhārat-māta kī jai* ('May Mother India/Bhārat be victorious') and *vandé mātaram* ('Hail Mother') were both greetings among activists and battle cries. Reproductions, oleographs and calendars with the representation of woman as Mother India flooded the market from the beginning of the twentieth century. The map of the Indian peninsula is such that it was possible to inscribe within its outline the standing figure of a woman – dressed in saffron, holding various items in her hands: the Congress flag, garland of *rudrākśa* beads, trident, book (all symbolising different aspects, desired characteristics or achievements).[23]

Vandé mātaram was a refrain from the Bengali novel (translated in many Indian languages) *Anandamath* (1882), by Bankim Chandra Chatterjee. In the days when various intellectuals in India were articulating anti-colonial sentiments, Chatterjee had fully elaborated in the novel

Bhārat-mātā by Abanindranath Tagore; Saraswati (seen in the film) by Raj Ravi Varma

the analogy between the nation and the goddess Durga, who rides on a lion and slays demons.[24] Painter Abanindranath's *Mother India* image was very popular among the middle class – an ascetic woman figure but also a composite goddess form, with iconographies borrowed both from Lakshmi (cloth, corn and lotus) and Saraswati (prayer beads and book).

The increase in narrative significance of the mother and the disappearance of the father in *Mother India* is better understood in terms of the long history of representation in Indian literature of male subjectivity in crisis. Underlining the story of Durga is the obvious meta-narrative of the helplessness of the pantheon of male gods to curb various *asuras*. Questions of male fertility and virility, physical health and deformity loom large in the epic *Mahābhārat*. The examples are numerous.

Leaders have spoken of the sense of emasculation men felt at the hands of foreign rulers (not only the British, but also the Portuguese, French and Dutch).[25] Contemporary scholars have pointed out that the changes the country was undergoing, the way local economies were affected by two global wars and put into further disarray by foreign rulers and local agencies alike, were often incomprehensible to common people. To make matters worse, indigenous usurers thrived under colonial rule. Money, debt, loss of control of means of production, corruption and spiritual bankruptcy are repeated literary and later cinematic motifs.

There are frequent representations of men frustrated in their efforts, unable to cope with situations, losing out to a stronger father or society. One consequence of this widespread disempowerment, according to scholars such as Partho Chatterjee, was that Indian men looked for a sense of comfort and control in the home environment. When Shyamu leaves, he is denied his home and the sacred hearth he lorded over. In the context of the representation of male failure, the depiction of female subjectivity becomes complicated and troublesome.

As the shooting progressed, Mehboob overshot his budget and took out further loans. A list from a 1956–7 file contains sources and amounts borrowed, but this one list cannot give the whole picture. Shaukat Khan says the actual figure of expense and debt was larger than the files suggest; he points out that this must have affected the way Mehboob altered the character of Lala as compared to that in *Aurat*. Not only was Mehboob forever plagued by debts and financial insecurity, he was not always in good health. 'Our father was a *foodie*,' says Shaukat Khan. Hard work combined with gourmandism and financial worries; and throughout the period of the making of *Mother India*, Mehboob was troubled by bouts of illness. Most letters of that period bear witness to people's anxious enquiry. I see Radha as Mehboob's *alter ego*, one who is untouched by bodily demands or troubles. Her *beauty* is an index to her psychic as well as physical strength – the *outer* being the showcase for the *inner*. Radha is constantly troubled, hungry, etc.; but she also emerges unflaggingly out of every type of situation.

Of course the spirit of reformation, nationalism and the fight for freedom did give rise to strong and positive heroes in cinema in India. Films of the 1930s and 40s portray patriarchs, feudal overlords, monarchs and saints. These characters are community-builders, lawmakers, lovers, protectors of family and community. They are, in short, role models – men operating equally well at home and in the public sphere, determined as well as compassionate – 'harder than even thunder; softer than even a flower' (*bajrādapi kathorāṇi mṛduṇi kusumādapi*). And there are films based on biographies or hagiographies. It is crucial to investigate properly why such characterisations seem almost to disappear from the cinema in the period after independence – especially during the Nehruvian era, when the euphoria of development swept the newly independent nation.

. . . .

Lala now openly suggests Radha should become his mistress. He comes to return the ox in exchange for her ultimate submission. If she complies he will exempt her debt and get back her land. Birju talks happily to the ox, 'You must never leave us.' Animals are as much part of the family in a household of farmers as humans are. Beginning with Radha as a bride, her head ornaments resembling those cows wear, all *Mother India*'s family members have been equated and associated with cows and oxen. But Radha is unshaken in her refusal and Lala leaves with a threat, 'Now you do not like the *deal* I am offering, you will see reason soon enough.' He does not use physical force, does not touch her even – only offers a *business transaction*.

Mother and son sing a song full of and moral aspiration, hope and determination in the face of adversity (*duniyā mein hum āyé hain to*) – a tremendously popular song:

> If we have come into this world, we must go on living.
> Even if life is poison, we must drink it.
> However many times we might fall, we will stand up again.
> We will walk through fire, even when burnt.

If film narratives show why and how something happens, songs tell us what we feel or how we could feel. Cinema raises feelings buried within psychic levels; songs voice them, helping the audience to come to terms with or sublimate them. The last possession an impoverished family holds on to is *dignity*; and it falls on women to guard that on behalf of family and community. Women, indeed, come to signify that last possession. The song continues, 'A true woman carries upon her the burden of shame of the entire world. Her modesty is her *dharma* [her rule of conduct, life's imperative].' It ends with an un-gendered aspiration, 'Those who have lived with dignity will die with dignity, too.' But Radha does not know how precariously close she is to losing even this last possession.

'This is not *lyric* but a *lecture*! Did you find it difficult to set these rhetorical sentences to a melody?' I asked, when I interviewed Naushad. In both Hindu and Islamic religious traditions, songs are discursive or narrative – and not merely lyrical. They tell stories, discuss ethical and philosophical issues. 'This was not unusual for me', Naushad replied. 'It can be described as a melodious way of rendering a discourse – not the same as a *pure song*.'

That the makers of this film were engaged with several thematic discursive elements is amply evident from the synopsis and the publicity brochure. The synopsis expands, 'What man could not do, Nature attempts.' The film has two villains, not just one: Man and Nature. Just as new saplings come out and Radha and Kamala are hopeful of a good harvest, the weather takes a turn for the worse. There is a storm, then torrential rains and ultimately a flood. The sequence begins in the studio. Pāndurang-carpenter described to me some of the process of filming the flood sequences: for example, they built mud huts on stilts. The studio would be flooded; a team of carpenters would get into the water while holding their breath, wait for the cue from the director and then cut the stilts, making the houses collapse. Kamala is with Radha on this fateful night; she is swept away with the newborn infant in her arms and cannot save him. Radha stands the rest of the night in waist-deep water holding aloft a bamboo platform, keeping her three remaining sons above the waters. Water snakes swim around them; Birju is not afraid of snakes. Later on in the film, we will see him carrying snakes on his person: both an ascetic and sexual symbol.

The third son dies that night. In the wake of death and destruction Sukhi-lala comes like a vulture, and Radha holds out her dead infant before him (partly in accusation and partly to seek help in giving it last rites). The dialogue written for Lala in this scene was originally extremely cruel and dark. 'What, you are giving me a corpse? Had you also given some gold on his neck or wrist, I could have considered taking it.' This dialogue was censored, but we see Sukhi-lala continue to mock her, addressing her as a queen, and renews his deal; he also offers false sympathy and some gram for the starving children. Radha commands her sons not to touch the gram and Ramu, her elder son, obeys silently. But when Birju sees their mother has kept an empty pot on the fire to fool them into believing there is food, he defies her and takes the gram from Lala's proffered hands. But no sooner has he begun to chew on them, he spits them out. Lala returns furious. Birju succumbs to hunger and exposure, and faints. Crazed with grief and helplessness, Radha hunts for the gram on the floor. Radha has always worked in mud with dignity. Today, it is not mud but indignity that covers her body completely.

This is a *cinema of excess*. The flood scene with all its fury and melodrama prepares the audience for what is to come. Interestingly, the censor board had deleted what actually was to follow: 'Sequence where villagers approach Lala for relief but he refuses to come to their rescue (96 feet in reel 10).' Fortunately two production stills of the deleted footage are preserved. At several moments in the history of British India, the country had experienced *man-made* famines caused by the administration as well as natural ones – particularly during the two world wars, when food was sent to British and allied forces across the globe and very little was kept for home consumption. *Aurat* refers to that history

Villagers demand Sukhi-
lala should release food
grain: from a scene
deleted by the censors

and has Bansi leading villagers in protest against Lala. It is interesting to note that the government of independent India deemed the representation of an irate mob confronting an unscrupulous trader unsuitable for public viewing. When the censor enforced the deletions Mehboob resisted and the censor certificate – issued on 7 July 1957 – carries a triangular mark, denoting the decision was carried out despite the director's protest.

Mehboob had enlarged a photograph of himself and Prime Minister Nehru (along with Sajid) and made it into a coloured litho-print that still

adorns the office wall. A caption below proclaims, 'A colourful romance of the soil, presenting a heroic solution to our food problem'. India's food problem had not improved much with independence and India had seen the government's inability to compel hoarders to release hoarded food grain, a bungling and corrupt public food-distribution system, and subsequently, Nehru asking America for food assistance and the introduction of the PL 480, people's immense dissatisfaction at substandard wheat (introduced even

Sardar Akhtar, Sajid and Mehboob with Nehru

in regions where it was not part of the staple diet). *Grow More Food* was an important national campaign and agenda for India's first two five-year plans.

The intended sequence definitely would have better explained the way the story now develops. When the men of the village fail to secure food, Radha steps into the rich man's house to accept and finalise the *deal* in exchange for food for her sons. In this, perhaps the most discussed sequence of *Mother India*, the mythological material used up till now is taken to another limit. Sukhi-lala welcomes Radha, gleefully addressing her as 'Lakshmi', winding a gold chain around her neck over and over again. Playing on his name, he adds, 'I even tie my dog with golden chains. If one holds Sukhi-lala's hands, one is sure to be *happy* [*sukhi*].' Since she has been equated with goddesses, the desecration of her body will be that much more poignant to the audience. In a remarkable shot Lala is made to look puny before the regally erect Radha: even in her fall the peasant woman towers over the trader.

The sacred and the profane clash and combine with terrible effects now. Prominent in the house is a wooden seat with a statuette of Lakshmi. Radha gives vent to her anger at the goddess, 'Mother, you did not feel shame appearing as me, watch me now robbed of my shame and honour. Don't laugh! You might be able to support the entire universe, but try taking care of children. Become a mother first, then see how even your steps falter!' (Interestingly, all three goddesses associated with Radha are childless, but are addressed as mothers.) Radha's face, held in a remarkable close-up as she cautions the goddess not to laugh at her fall, is red with anger and passion (reddened with extra make-up). It fills the screen, the image photographed with a wide-angled lens, the camera placed low, the whole scene lit up from below – the face is indeed *terrible*. Anil Mehta remarks with a note of regret, 'We do not frame heroines' faces quite in this manner these days. Whatever be the situation they are made *glamorous* – using the normal lens, choosing the best possible angle.' Nargis is supposed to have objected to Radha speaking that way to a goddess; but, once he had made a decision, Mehboob would not budge. Disconcerted by this unusual tirade Sukhi-lala wants to remove the deity from the scene and what Radha does now must have sent shivers down the spines of many women – and men. Radha stops Lala from taking the goddess away; if she has to engage in a sexual act, the goddess must remain and *watch the horrible fun*.[26]

A look into past narratives, mythologies and beliefs concerning gods and goddesses can help us appreciate the different ways these are appropriated and subverted in this film. The earth or *bhumi* is where one resides and grows grain; it is *wealth* – like a *milch cow*. Early in the history of civilisation, *terra firma* is non-moveable, non-transferable property, forever attached to a person or family. She is 'all-bearing, good-holding, firm-standing' [*acalā, sthirā*], she 'does-not-follow-after-anyone'.[27] With the rise of the trading class, the concepts of *wealth* and *prosperity* are more and more attached to Śri and then Lakshmi; Mother Earth is subsumed and latent in the worship of the latter. Realisations that land, as well as houses and crops, are transferable or *moveable* property, that wealth can so easily be lost, grow acute with increased trade and sea-faring activity; and Lakshmi acquires the epithet *cancalā* or fickle. More and more, land and wealth are both homologised as women; they are to be possessed – kept as possessions. There was a resurgence of this sort of ideology during the period of nationalism, when middle-class women were required to be Lakshmi-wives (as Dipesh Chakravarty has pointed out).

Sukhi-lala is a successful trader and Lakshmi is stably installed in his house. Similarly he wants to *keep* Radha and not just *rape* her – the two are very different expressions of power, possession and oppression. But because of Radha the seat of the Lakshmi in his house is displaced – something that is sure to bring down bad fortune. Radha is completely covered with mud and muck and yet Sukhi-lala says she is 'as beautiful as Lakshmi'. This is not incongruous for Nargis is truly splendid. Nargis was not conventionally beautiful. Physical beauty in *Mother India* seems not to be attached to a single source, the persona of the star, but dispersed, imbuing the whole narrative, emanating from it. Those present during shooting remember her as a woman possessed, taking mud and make-up and applying them to herself over and over again. It is mind-boggling to imagine how many times the actress had to do so, or stand, lie and roll in mud and muck. It is often asked why or how the figure of the heroine exudes such sexuality in this sequence. The answer is connected with the narrative choice of Shyamu's disappearance over death. Radha is never away from the memory and desires of conjugal life. The farmer's wife remains the object of the trader's desire. Before succumbing to the man's offer, Radha had thrown her black thread *mangal-sūtra* on the ground. She must deny her belief in Shyamu's continuing existence if she has to engage in a sexual act with this man.

And before that, Lala forces the deity and the wooden seat away. Radha falls on the ground sobbing and finds the necklace back in her hand. Taking this to be a sign her husband is alive, her determination returns and she tries to leave the house. Lala forces himself on her and the censor intervenes again, removing shots 'where scuffle of Radha and Lala is shown after he has caught her in his hands'. Radha pushes Sukhilala on a heap of cotton and he is blinded for a while. Then she beats him with a stick; Lala thereafter is a *lame man* – signifying the loss of virility.

So the film critiques something it has been using till now: the imagery of Lakshmi. The plethora of mythical references and iconography notwithstanding, the film is radical in comparison with *Aurat*, where characters attribute misfortunes to destiny and *karma* and pray in a temple for relief. There Radha escapes Sukhi-lala only because the roof falls on him at that precise moment. Another divine intervention follows immediately after Radha's escape – rain brings relief from drought. In *Mother India*, there is no representation of Radha or the people praying to any tutelary god or goddess, even at times of extreme adversity. Then again, Radha can scold goddess Lakshmi *because* she (and the narrative) is within the tradition of *Bhakti* – the popular form of personal worship and devotion (extant since the eleventh century). A mortal getting the better of a god, taking a goddess to task, rebuking her for a breach of promise are familiar *Bhakti* narratives. But this is the last use of the Lakshmi motif, as the film moves towards more nationalist and contemporary discourse.

. . . .

Radha returns home and boils her sons a yam she has found in the fields. The scene ends with an extraordinary image in extreme long shot: Radha and her sons get down to restore the ravaged earth under a violently colourful sky at dusk. As was the common practice of the time, Mehboob seldom used exterior establishing shots, before going indoors and shooting a film entirely in the studio. He often used painted backdrops and skies, making no effort to go outdoors. This image reminiscent of that earlier practice was shot on location, with a heavily painted glass held in front of the camera. The *dramatic sky* occupies most of the frame; Radha and her two sons are tiny specks, forlorn figures amid destruction and damage.

The next shot is equally impressive. Radha's face fills the screen; through a long dissolve we begin to see small figures, a procession of villagers in carts, lining the bottom frame. The dissolve is achieved within the camera by alternately masking or matting the bottom and upper half of the frame – the matting line horizontally dividing the frame is clearly visible. With the dawning of the next day, there begins a mass exodus of villagers, echoing the timeless practice of evacuating settlements after large-scale natural calamities such as famine or flood.[28]

Kamala asks Radha to leave; Radha breaks into a song, making an appeal to the people to stay on. 'O you, departing ones! Do not leave your homes. Your Mother is calling out with folded hands [*o jānéwālé*].' While conveying the situation to Badayuni and Naushad, Mehboob had specified that the song should be able to evoke the event of partition. Millions had been displaced as a result of the formation of India and Pakistan; over a million had died in riots. It is awesome to see the submerged land and hundreds of villagers assembled for the shot. The plea in the song is caught in a time warp, impossible to respond to – nothing can actually be revised. But the impact of this plea, *don't leave*, would sear the minds and hearts of Indian audiences or anyone else who has known migration and exile. The appeal includes people outside the village – outside the narrative – encompassing cities and townships. 'Where would you go, leaving all this behind – these cities, roads, tenements? Maybe this land is spoilt just now; but you can never be happy anywhere in the world, if you break mother's heart.' The villagers halt, listen and stay on. If there had been a near obsessive representation of urban migration in films from the 1930s through to the 50s, *Mother India* is unique in that it portrays a reversal of the process of migration and a desire to arrest, as it were, an event that has already happened.

As a surprising testimony to the support Mehboob was able to muster from the local people while shooting outdoors, a farmer had agreed to flood his 500 acres of cultivated land for this scene. Awe is writ large in the eyes of Surendra and Sajid as they stare at an actual deluge. The last page of the publicity booklet says, 'When a producer requires 300 bullock carts, 200 farmers, scores of horses, tractors, ploughs and 500 acres of paddy fields to be flooded – not to mention the sympathy and active support of scores of villages – to produce a spectacular picture like "Mother India", money becomes a helpless instrument of negotiation.' It is amazing to think that a farmer had actually offered or agreed to this for the purpose of a film; one wonders how long it was before the land became cultivable again. There is a belief that the villagers did not take money; the carts, horses, tractors were made freely available. However, account books reveal the villagers were indeed paid for their services (of course their hospitality and cooperation went beyond any financial transaction). It would have been impossible to use so much of the village resources without some payment.

It is well known that studio films in India generally contain over half a dozen songs. But when it comes to song-picturisation accompanying tragic moments, the practice comes under greater scrutiny. Some viewers think songs halt narration and feel irritation at such apparent excess. However, let us explore this particular sequence. If Radha were to approach each family (even a few represented ones) with her plea to stay on, there would have had to be an inordinate amount of dialogue, emotion and rhetoric. That could hardly be contained in three minutes of film time. Songs can economise on film time or stretch it; we see instances of both in this film.

The villagers stay on and work hard to restore the land. The mother and her young sons work in knee-deep mud, shovelling away dead stalks, and pulling the plough. Radha slips and the boys try in vain to lift her up. When they succeed – they have turned into young men. Dissolves achieved through the camera need discipline and meticulous prior organisation. The younger actors are shown helping Radha; the camera is rewound and brought to the desired moment where the dissolve is to start; the older actors replace the younger ones, maintaining exactly the prior composition – the camera is run again. Young Ramu and Birju pull the plough while Radha feeds them; there is no time to stop for food and rest. They are quite prosperous now and have acquired oxen for the plough and a cart to ride on.

Another song, the antithesis of the first one, immediately follows this hyphen-like section in the middle of the film. The joyous song proclaims, 'Sorrow-filled days are over and happy days are here, O brother! Our new life is tinged with new colours [*dukh bharé din bité ré bhaiyā*].' Close-ups of the rotating wheel of the family cart evoke a popular Sanskrit aphorism: *Cakravat parivartante sukhāni ca duhkhāni ca* ('Like wheels, rotate happinesses and sorrows'). The song plays with time and space, going back to those happy days with Shyamu. Today's happiness brings back happy memories of yesteryears. The family is at a village fair; Shambhu and Kamala are with Shyamu's family. Precocious little Birju dances as a crowd gathers around. The shots are from a sequence conceived and shot for the earlier half of the film, but only these fragments were retained – inserted within this song sequence.

. . . .

A new stanza begins with a young woman swinging and singing. Ramu is with her – he has found a sweetheart. In order to avoid any jerkiness, a makeshift platform was attached to the swing to accommodate Irani and the Debrie camera. During one take the ropes snapped; Irani fell and broke his arm. His first concern was for his favourite camera, which had broken in the fall and had to be replaced by a Mitchell. Irani called the Mitchell a 'blind' or *andhā*-camera, because after setting up an exposure the cameraman had to operate while looking through a separate viewfinder. He preferred to look through the camera lens proper, while taking a shot, and adjusting continuously. The song ends with mother and sons looking skyward – their faces aglow with hope and confidence, framed by sickles. And then a crane shot creates a startling image: stacks of hay outline the map of pre-Partition India, peopled by dancing villagers. India was celebrating the tenth anniversary of its freedom in 1957 and the country was preparing for a celebration. The title and the film inspired feelings of patriotism in everyone associated with its production; Mehboob was also keen to profit by releasing *Mother India* that year on 15 August, Independence Day. That could not be achieved in the end but the publicity campaign for the film was launched on that day by Radio Ceylon (popular for its Indian film music programme *Binaca Geetmala*).

The image of Radha with her plough, strong, beautiful and earthy, formed the centrepiece of the main publicity poster. Throughout India the plough is considered to be male; its image here is clearly phallic. Radha's sexuality is accentuated as she is caught in dynamic diagonal compositions, the plough by her side. Male and female principles are harnessed together successfully for the purpose of creation. Sukhi-lala tells Radha, 'You have changed the village beyond recognition.'

Radha's sons are as different now as they had been in childhood. The obedient son Ramu has turned into a good farmer, played by Rajendra Kumar, a refugee from Pakistan. He was still employed as a police sub-inspector and a newcomer to the industry (he had acted in Mehboob's *Āwāz*). For *Mother India*, Rajendra Kumar received an augmented salary of 5,000 rupees. Raaj Kumar, acting as Shyamu, received 6,000. The actors' contract stipulated that they should receive ten per cent of the total amount as a monthly salary (for ten months). Unfortunately, the file containing the correspondence with Nargis cannot be traced, but it is widely remembered that she, by comparison, received 5,000 rupees per month. Naushad's contract is unavailable, but records show Ali Raza was to be paid 20,000 rupees. It is interesting to note the remunerative equity achieved by Nargis in a film industry that still pays actresses appreciably less than their male counterparts.

Sunil Dutt, the actor playing Birju, was in pain, his legs in casts following a helicopter accident, the evening I interviewed him. An hour and a half later I asked him, in view of his discomfort, if we should stop. 'I don't feel tired when I speak of Mehboob-Sāb', he had replied. Speaking with Sunil Dutt and others, images of Mehboob Khan and the environment he created in the studio emerge clearly – a world containing

The old and the young: Rajendra Kumar and Sunil Dutt carry Surendra and Sajid

a *good patriarch*, equally loved and feared (besides Sab or Saheb, Mehboob was also addressed widely as Baba or father). To understand *Mother India* and its principal characters, we need to combine our understandings of two slightly different concepts: hero and patriarch.

With one film behind him, Dutt was working in a municipal bus depot and occasionally as an announcer for Radio Ceylon, when Muqri took him to Mehboob. Asked to wait and hang around, Dutt was content simply to be inside Mehboob Studios. After Partition, his family had continued as agriculturists in India (with the help of a land grant from the new government), and so Dutt closely identified with the story of the film, which he managed to glean from unit members. Curious and friendly by nature, he spoke to whomever he could and discovered the studio's precarious financial situation. Dutt says he offered to work for free; there is no contract in his name, only records of him receiving small amounts (ten or twelve rupees), drawn from petty cash, during outdoor shooting.

The characterisation of Birju is complex, touched with ambivalence and confusion. Dutt's task was made more difficult as he was instructed to observe and incorporate some of Sajid's mannerisms and gestures, so that Birju's transition from childhood to youth would appear credible. Birju has grown up to be obsessive in his hatred towards Sukhi-lala; he is moody and undisciplined, quick to pick a fight. As in the case of the childhood sequence, young Birju sprawls luxuriantly on a heap of grain, as the yield is particularly good that year. Reluctant to give Lala his share, Birju insists on seeing the account books. But what good is that if he cannot read? He appeals to the villagers, mostly illiterate, in vain. 'What, you too have given your thumb prints without reading what is written in the ledgers!' he fumes. Shambhu informs him that even his grandmother had done the same: misfortune has come to them in a *traditional* way. But Birju will not give in so easily; and scared of this macho man with a temper, Lala commands his armed goons to take on Birju. Radha appeals on behalf of her son, while Ramu can only mutter, 'If Lala has rights over his share, we must give him what is due to him.'

. . . .

There is one person in the village Birju respects and that is Chandra, the schoolmaster's daughter. Birju sits among young kids in a class she is teaching. But all he knows are the vowels, which he repeats and bird-calls in the soundtrack mimic that sound. The suggestion is that Birju is raw and primitive – like the vowels. Chandra scolds him, 'Why did you not come all these months? Don't you want to progress beyond the vowels? All you know beyond them are all sorts of misdeeds: teasing girls, breaking their pots, gambling!' Birju has taken to bad ways; but he is different with her. He would like to come to her, learn the consonants and all; but feels inhibited, for Chandra is educated and he is not.[29] He likes her very much, finds her 'better than all the other girls of the village'. Chandra *is* different, imaged differently. The clothes she wears are not the dark, deep hue of village cotton but pale (clothes with synthetic dyes were allotted to her), mostly blue or white. Her natural pale complexion is accentuated by her stillness.

The village school

Birju wants study to have access to the 'cruel knowledge' or *ẓālim vidyā* contained in Sukhi-lala's ledgers. The knowledge the British have brought is powerful but obscure; it has replaced all traditional knowledge, 'even that contained in the Vedas'. The film discourse is replete with such references to education – an important factor in the widespread disempowerment felt by Indian men at the time. Mehboob Khan himself, incapable of composing letters in English, would dictate letters in Gujarati to his staff; they would then be composed and read out for his approval. Later, he would put his signatures (in English) on the final copy typed on official stationery. Though much aware of it, Mehboob was not inhibited by the fact that he spoke broken English and he could spend hours conversing with film personnel, ministers and government officials, as well as people from all walks of life visiting the studio. He met people and entertained widely during his travels. Acquaintances describe Mehboob as speaking with slow deliberation, and as a former professional actor, acting out his thoughts; his guests listened, captivated.[30] The matter of education would be a deep concern all his life and he donated generously to educational initiatives. And rather than entering the film business, he was keen for his sons to study extensively.

Chandra informs Birju that those ledgers contain anything but *vidyā* and using stones as a teaching aid explains how Sukhi-lala has been tricking them for over twenty years. They continue to pay accumulated interest so that the initial loan inflates to many times its original amount. The censored sequence of the villagers' protest corroborates how strongly the film team felt about the issue of education and knowledge: a print of painter Ravi Varma's image of Saraswati hangs on Sukhi-lala's wall. Not only the goddess of wealth but also the goddess of learning is in Lala's possession.

. . . .

Several visual and narrative tropes combine to transform Birju into a romantic outlaw. But initially he is a tease, flirting with the village women, breaking their water pots when they fetch water from the well or the river – recalling Krishna's early life in the village of Vṛndāvan. The girls take their complaints to Radha; they line up in single-file and one by one they tell her how many of their pots Birju has broken with his sling-shot. An element of humour tellingly intrudes here. Disappointed, one girl laments, 'Aunt, Birju has *not* broken even a single pot of mine!'[31] Obviously, the girls are amorously drawn towards this unusual youth and their feelings are consequently ambivalent. Birju's behaviour is explained in terms of his tangled feelings towards Lala's daughter Rupa, on the one hand, and his uncomplicated affection for Chandra, on the other. The publicity booklet bears a caption beneath a painting of the village girls, 'There is more mischief in the village than comes to our ears … . Presence of a ruthless moneylender in the village irritated his [Birju's] keen sense of justice. And so did the tantalizing tricks on Sukhi-lala's proud daughter, who went out of her way to tease Birju. Rupa and Birju were thus natural enemies.' Rupa, the mortal-Lakshmi in the house of the moneylender, is fickle and vain. The first time we see her, Radha's bracelets are on her wrists. Birju is angry, but Rupa dismisses him, 'These belong to my father now and I will wear them.'

Ramu has chosen for his bride-to-be Shambhu's niece, Champā, whom the childless couple has adopted. Ramu and Champa have been meeting in the fields, for they are not supposed to be together before they are wed. Mehboob's attempts to make the film commercially successful come into full force in the song-and-dance picturisations in the latter half of the film. Notably, the two sets of song-and-dance sequences – those with Radha and Shyamu and those with the younger generation – differ in style and content. The theme of work is predominant in the earlier set, whereas the scenes involving the younger generation foreground love and sexuality. The earlier imaginative use of two-shot compositions gives way entirely to an editing pattern with shot counter-shot and eyeline matching. The gaze is *male*: Ramu looks on as Champa dances for his pleasure – and the audience's. Actress Kumkum playing Champa dances to a song (based on the semi-classical *dādra* form from Benaras): 'I will not remove the veil covering my face [*ghunghat nahī kholungī*]!' The earlier attention to the conventions of realism is discarded, except

Ramu and Champa swing and sing

for one detail: orphan Champa wears torn and faded clothes.

Radha wants both her sons to be married and approaches the schoolmaster for his consent to Chandra's marriage with Birju. The man has heard about Birju's waywardness and so refuses but he mentions something that reinforces how richly detailed the narrative is. Chandra came to him at the time when her entire family was swept away in the flood; he cannot jeopardise the happiness of this girl he has ever since cared for. Chandra and Champa are both reared by foster parents. Rupa too has no mother and hence belongs to a broken family unit. Shyamu's father is already dead, when the film begins. Radha's family is the most intact, although her parents are only shown in a single inserted shot and later her husband abandons her. Memories of Partition fill Indian films with representations of fractured families.

Birju is despondent and tells Chandra, 'I wanted to marry only you; now I will never marry.' Chandra's reply is of tremendous significance: 'You *are* married, Birju, to the land of this village. *She* is your *bride*, but Sukhi-lala has abducted her. Won't you free her from him?' This short scene is enacted in a low key – so unobtrusively that one hardly notices or remembers it. This was actress Āzrā's debut role; reviewers and industry observers had described her unfairly as 'wooden'. But her flat mode of delivering the dialogues helps cut down on the melodrama that would have been inevitable otherwise. Chandra is the opposite of Rupa, who is coquettish, wild and tempestuous. Chanchal, sister of the great star Madhubala, was borrowed for the role of Rupa from Madhubala Productions, which her father ran (he took 100 rupees as 'token money').

. . . .

Birju sells some cotton to another trader, a new arrival in the area, who is trying to compete with Lala on the sly. With the money, Birju buys a pair of *kangan* for his mother, similar to those Sukhi-lala has taken away; and this time they are of gold. But in order not to get into trouble with her, Birju makes up a cock-and-bull story about meeting a holy man with miraculous powers. He had asked the *sādhu* for the bangles which the man materialised out of thin air. Radha is initially happy when Birju puts them on her, but is later frantic: 'Why did you ask for these? Why not for your father's whereabouts?' At that moment Ramu returns home with the oxen and Radha begins to hallucinate, seeing Shyamu in the person of Ramu. Shyamu for her is incarnated in *both* her sons.

Ramu sees this is as nothing but theft on the part of Birju and the brothers begin to quarrel. Lala comes and takes away the bangles: the cotton was from his part of the share and so he has sole rights over them. Defeated, Birju takes leave of the village, singing a song that was tremendously popular with the youth of the time: 'Neither am I a God, nor a Satan. Whatever the world might consider me to be, I am just a man [*nā main bhagawān hun, nā śaitān hun*].' When one leaves the pale of the society one has two options. Birju first seeks the company of ascetics, but finds only a set of no-good, hashish-smoking idlers. Birju's attire of a black blanket invokes various austere religious orders.[32]

Before Birju follows the other alternative, there is Ramu's wedding. In a magnificent scene, scores of carts set out for the wedding – and there is a bullock-cart race. Birju and Rupa are on separate carts, with their respective male and female friends; they sing a song with the refrain, 'O driver, drive slowly [*gādiwālé gādi*]' – a remarkable composition of onomatopoeic sounds and lyrical words, with plain speech breaking in between. This is one time when Birju and Rupa flirt happily.

Champa enters the house of Radha as a new bride. These scenes recall the time Radha and Shyamu were newly-weds; but these are pale shadows of those early passages. Champa becomes a mother, Radha a grandmother, Ramu a father and Birju an uncle. Every birth means another new relationship. Every birth is connected with the harvest season and this one with Holi, the colour festival. Coming after harvest, it is a time for joy, for celebrating the bounties of nature at Spring; it is also a time for expressing bawdy, vulgar feelings and acting out sexual excesses – a Saturnalia of sorts. Holi provides Hindi films with another pretext for visual extravaganza, song and dance. Mehboob had asked his old friend Sitara Devi to appear once again in his film and initiate the sequence. She makes a very brief appearance dressed as a male dancer. Rupa is happy because Birju is dancing close to her, but does not know his attention is riveted not upon her but the bangles on her wrists. She wants him to drench her with coloured festival water. But Birju pours colours on Chandra, who is standing as if petrified – a statue carved out of stone. She knows this loveplay is leading nowhere; Birju cannot ultimately bring colour to her life.

Birju loses all interest in the festival and snatches the bangles away from Rupa. She cries out and Birju's action is interpreted as a violation of her honour. His family tries to defend him to the irate villagers. Taking advantage of the situation Sukhi-lala insults the family in public: 'If Radha wants to wear *kangans*, tell her to come to me. I will give her as many as she wants.' Only Kamala protests and warns, 'Lala, don't make me open my mouth, lest I expose you. Know this is your sins visiting you and you deserve to have a daughter like Rupa.' The event ends in a general free-for-all and Birju gets seriously beaten up.

Birju must become an outlaw now and steals a gun. Radha spots him hiding it and pleads with him: 'The gun will never feed a mouth, cover the head of a woman, produce crop. What good is the gun?' These sentiments against armed violence come from Radha and not Ramu. Childhood affection forgotten, Ramu and Birju engage in a fight that ends up in them seriously hurting each other. The family tries to separate the two and Birju perceives himself as alienated from his own family as well as the community. Radha, fallen on the ground, catches hold of his feet, trying to stop him leaving the house. The censor allowed the director to leave in only 'flash shots' of this scene, showing the collapse of family values and the degradation of Radha. In all, a total of 237 feet were removed from *Mother India*.

Birju was shot at when he was stealing the gun. The villagers spot blood on Radha's hands and accuse her of sheltering a criminal son. At dusk, Sukhi-lala incites the villagers to set fire to the haystacks where Birju is hiding. Radha runs wildly between burning haystacks calling out 'Birju! Birju!' The scene is protracted; the call is repeated over and over again. Mehboob took shots from every possible angle and distance. Once again, Irani works wonders with his camera. In his *Filmfare* award (1958) acceptance speech, Irani spoke of his theories about colour photography: 'In depicting atmosphere in black and white, you achieve an approximation. You can never capture the vividness of the pink dawn skies, the orange of the rising sun or mellow twilight. In the fire scene of *Mother India*, I found I could get the colour of fire and smoke by using different filters. In fact some of the changes of colour became so violent I had to reduce yellow, black and red.' Normally, in the dramatic sequences of their black-and-white films, Irani and Mehboob preferred off-centre, angular, expressionistic images. Colour could be seen as adding weight or mass to images; so in this film we mostly see centred, well-balanced images. At the same time, Irani does not always bother to give the images picture postcard-like perfection. The stylistic differences between Irani–Mehboob's black-and-white films and their colour ones merit further study.

The fire scene was shot in the village of Umra at a farm belonging to one Ishwardās Nemāni. The film and its making had inspired this farmer to compose a booklet of poems, *Radha*, that makes reference to the scene being shot by the river Ambika. Shooting carried on for a week. Sunil Dutt recounts how initially a girl from the village, doubling for Nargis, had been injured; not wanting to endanger another, Nargis insisted on doing the scene herself. On 1 March 1957, Nargis got trapped in the flames when a wind suddenly spread the fire beyond control. Sunil Dutt rushed to save her and both received burns. All accounts speak of a romance developing between the stars after this event. Whatever the exact sequence of events, Nargis and Sunil Dutt married after the release of the film, on 11 March 1958. Mehboob was worried that a marriage between Nargis and her on-screen son would be unacceptable to audiences who identify actors with characters they play. But the success of the film was a secured fact. It was also a marriage between a Muslim woman and a Hindu man. The Bombay film industry was an oasis of communal harmony in the post-Partition period – it remains largely so even now.

The female Earth remains *grounded* no matter how cruelly she is visited by rain or fire – *parjanya* and *agni* – both anthropomorphised as male. Collecting water can be a pleasurable and communal activity (popular representations vastly romanticise this form of work): it is arduous if the land is arid or if there is a drought (as in *Aurat*). Getting wet in the rain is romantic; for farmers, rains are the wedding of mother-earth and father-rain. But torrential rain and flood are damaging to people and crops. Similarly, the fire burns comfortingly in the hearth, cooks a meal; it can also be cruel, destroying forests and huts. The publicity booklet comments, 'The lamp that lights a home often burns down the house.' Radha searches for her son, paying no heed to her own safety. Once, she had entered *figuratively* the fire of Sukhi-lala's lust, in order to save Birju from dying of hunger. Today, she enters the fire *literally* to save the perpetually precarious life of this son of hers. And again, it is only Birju who can and does save Radha from the fire. But

The bandits and the rocky land of vice

Yet another sequence that did not make it: Shyamu and Radha pawn the jewels

immediately afterwards in the dark of the night Birju leaves the village. Radha's song here, calling him back, is one instance of the melodramatic excess city audiences are uncomfortable about; I noticed this when I watched the film in a theatre in Pune.

. . . .

Birju gathers together a gang of bandits. They stop caravans entering and leaving the village, loot weddings (occasionally carrying the bride away, since it is time-consuming to strip a bride of her gold). One such caravan contains Chandra travelling with her groom. Birju lifts the pale veil covering her face with his gun; this very macho act gives way to gentleness as he covers her face again and allows her to go her way. Rupa too is to be married; Birju sends Sukhi-lala a letter, announcing a raid on the day of the wedding. Lala seeks Radha's help, falling at her feet, beseeching her as his 'sister'. 'Sister!' Kamala bursts out, 'Only a goddess is capable of such forgiveness; call her *mother* instead.' Radha responds to Sukhi-lala's plea and vows she would fight to protect the chastity of Rupa – this woman-of-the-village – as she had fought for her own.

On the day of Rupa's wedding, Radha takes out Birju's gun and intercepts the bandits when they arrive. Birju is extremely happy to see his mother, who pleads with him, 'I cannot live without you, Birju; they will kill you!' But this is a point of no return. Birju enters the house of Sukhi-lala and delivers a line that will be heard down decades of Hindi films, 'The law will not spare me; but [before that] I will not spare you.' Birju piles up the moneylender's ledgers and sets them on fire proclaiming, 'I have learnt all your evil knowledge, Lala!' And then, Birju kills Sukhi-lala, his lifelong enemy.

Ramu tries to explain to Birju his enmity is only with the father, not with the daughter, and Champa helps Rupa to hide. Beyond listening to any voice of sanity, Birju pulls her up on his horse and sets out to leave the village. All Radha's teaching, her words of non-violence, has been in vain. There is only one way she can stop him now. She takes aim and shoots at her son. Radha's stance is that of an American Western hero: legs apart, feet planted on the ground, head and gun held high. Birju falls to the ground and Rupa runs away without a glance at the fallen man. Birju struggles to sit up and holds out towards her the bangles he has retrieved earlier – the sign of all the rest, tangible and intangible, that will be returned to her, the house, the land and its yield, her honour and dignity. Once again the censor board intervened and deleted shots 'where wounded Birju holds out "Kangan" (61 feet)'. The authority displayed no objection to the representation of a parent killing a child; but, the depiction of an unruly criminal son as the only one capable of restoring Radha's dignity was clearly unacceptable. Or perhaps they saw the *kangan* only as a marital sign and were worried about the incestuous implications here. They would have been acutely aware of the fact that this son's name means the same as that of the father's. On the other hand, this representation might be one of the principal reasons for the film's popularity.

Mehboob edited his own films; critics have specially applauded his editing style from *Humāyun* onwards. A series of shot counter-shots follows now: Radha in mid-long shot, Birju in extreme long. With every return to Radha's image the camera cuts in slightly closer, her image growing slightly larger each time. Mehboob allots just enough time to the image of Radha for the audience to fully absorb what has transpired; and then they are returned to the familiar world of love between mother and son; a world that believes 'one can hurt only who one loves'.[33] Her body crumples; she drops the gun at the sight of her dying son offering her the bangles for the last time. Radha rushes to take Birju in her arms. The entire scene, moving from the mother and son meeting after a period of separation, to the crisis in that relationship, to her gunning him down and then this return to their final bonding, is a cinematic *tour de force*.

But the world is changed beyond recognition. Like a floodgate, the palm of Radha's hand tries vainly to stop the blood from flowing. Without any further melodrama, delay or dialogue, the scene dissolves to real floodgates opening to let out the water – but the water is blood red. The director cheats in the interests of grand symbolism, by inserting the image of a dam (Kākrāpar in Surat district, Gujarat), instead of the normal small sluice gate of a *nahar* or irrigation canal. This is not all.

Next is a high-angle shot: villagers line the sides of the canal and watch silently as the blood water begins to irrigate the green fields. The epic film evokes one of the hoariest civilisational acts of all: human sacrifice – conducted with the belief that it would help to contain or release water for the benefit of a community.

Radha's killing of Birju could be discussed within the context of western psychoanalytic discourse, in terms of the male fear of castration at the hands of the woman/mother (Rosie Thomas has initiated such a discussion). This representation, the annihilation of the disobedient son, might have had roots in the director's past. Elder members of the family recall Mehboob receiving corporal punishment from his father, when he escaped school to see films travelling companies brought to the village, or ran away to Bombay. But such explanations are valid when we identify only with the men (Birju or Shyamu). The Oedipal drama abounds in films in India, but, significantly, psychoanalytical explanations seem to tell only part of the story – one has then to locate other sources and material that structure the drama.

The structure of the film is interesting as it begins as a third-person account, objective and documentary-like; and immediately after, the subjectivity of the female protagonist takes over and initiates the narrative. In the main section, it is first the couple Shyamu and Radha, then Radha alone and lastly Birju and Radha who occupy the central position in the film – audience identification oscillates between these figures, whether alone or paired. However predominant the figure of Radha (or Birju) might be, the reception of *Mother India* cannot be explained in terms of a single character. In addition, each character develops and come to represent different individual and communal virtues, and addresses different viewers in different ways. The subjectivity of each could be discussed in terms of his or her individual self, his or her relation with the immediate family and with the village community. Individualism and community, modernity and tradition are often aligned along different poles; however, these are not perceived as mutually exclusive in India (and in many other societies), but as interlaced. And if these are not seen as contradictions, but necessary components of a personality (in any post-colonial situation) – at times at odds, at times in harmony with each other – the discussion shifts to grounds other than psychoanalysis.

Let me recall the end of *Aurat*. Tulsi, Champa, Ramu are all with Radha as Birju lies on her lap. In a montage style sequence, we see their faces separately and together – they experience the event individually and collectively. And then it is as if Radha sees her entire life pass before her eyes, in a collage of some earlier shots and some new ones. *Mother India*, on the other hand, begins thus – Radha looking back at the past, at 'what was there, before all this became possible'. At the end of the film, Radha looks forward to the benefits of development, her sacrifice now behind her. It is beyond the scope of this book to enquire into audiences' perceptions of the cost and result of their independence. But these perceptions must certainly have been roused by this sequence in the film.

In the very last shot, *Mother India* returns to 'present time', with a tight medium shot of Radha, Ramu and some villagers looking out of the frame. If Radha had singly initiated a look at the past, at pre-independence India, others have joined her now to look at an India after independence, at the signs of a progressing nation. What do they see; what lies ahead? There is no answer to that; the film ends here. Ramu had told Radha, 'The canal has *come* to the village' – development has come from the outside. Do they comprehend how this development came about, and from where? All the truly celebratory aspects of the film relate to the past; there is no celebration *after* the irrigation facility comes to the village – no song, no dance. This is not an untroubled representation of the nation.

The death of the darling son, the romantic hero Birju, could raise some questions, too: what does this lovable, anarchic-criminal hero-figure signify? What dies along with his death? Mehboob had designed an insignia for his company, an audiovisual sandwich. The visual image is that of the communist hammer and a sickle combined with Mehboob's initial 'M', over the production house's title. A soundtrack accompanies the visual (in voice-over by Mehboob's former music director, the poet Rafiq Ghaznavi): 'The Plaintiff might wish you a million ills, but what of it? That alone happens that God allows.'[34] In a 1957 article in *Filmfare*, Mehboob had tried to explain this incongruous juxtaposition of two different ideologies, one religious and the other Marxist, 'I took the hammer and sickle as our symbol, because we considered ourselves workers and not just producers, directors and stars. I have been accused of being a communist for using this symbol, but those who know me well, know that I am no communist.' Mehboob's films often depict non-conformity and unsanctioned behaviour, as part of social commentary. Birju is one of the most important, conspicuous instances of an anarchic character in his films, the only hero who neglects romantic love in the pursuit of social justice. However, his death reinforces the fact that representations of desire for protest and change in *popular* cinema in India have always given way to normalisation of the social order – to the

Mehboob's insignia

maintenance of the status quo. Then again, the censor board was there to erase even the hint of a desire for mass movement that Mehboob wanted inscribed in the film. In a deleted exchange between Radha and Birju, she was to tell him, 'Son, if you kill one Sukhi, another will be born.' Birju was to reply, 'Mother, if one Birju dies a thousand Birju will be born.' Mehboob had clashed with the censor throughout his career. *Elān* (1947) was banned outright for a period, because it seemed to support Quranic reforms for India. It was not only the Indian government that had such problems. The government in Turkey banned *Mother India* as a 'communist film'. Mehboob's insignia was excised from the print sent for Oscar nomination.

Gandhi's invocation of *rām rājya* or the rule-of-Ram as the ideal state and form of governance had roused the Indian people in vast numbers. The period of nationalism (and later decades) saw many a hero, a Ram or a Krishna, taking charge of the community. At the same time, several post-independence films were critical of the utopianism of this nationalist rhetoric, or saw *rām rājya* as an unrealised dream. In keeping with that viewpoint, throughout the film Ramu is shown as a less-than-attractive narrative agent, initiating nothing and achieving nothing. Interestingly, time and again, several writers and leaders in the years before independence, notably B. G. Tilak (1856–1920) and Bankim Chandra Chatterjee (1838–94), had attempted to turn Krishna into a political symbol relevant to modern India (ignoring the erotic aspects of this godhead). But, films in India have always shown Krishna as a prankster (a tradition established by D. G. Phalke in his silent film, *Śri Kṛṣṇa Janma* or *The Birth of Krishna*) or have drawn upon the popular topic of his adolescent erotic loveplay. Few films have dealt with the philosophical-political metaphors behind the life and acts of this godhead. However, it cannot be stated with any precision what the makers of this film had in mind when they showed Birju dying and Ramu enduring. Shyamu and Birju, separated by a generation, sharing the name of the same godhead, represent an ideal past and a troubled present. Birju makes it his life's mission to oppose the moneylender and does what Shyamu never dared, but he never gets what Shyamu had, namely a beautiful Lakshmi-wife. It will be profitable to study *Mother India* in this light – in this blurring of utopic and dystopic visions of India, past and present.[35]

The audio part of the insignia reflects Mehboob's religious nature, which is always alluded to in stories about him. P. K. Nair recalls how the director would spread a mat in the garden – out in the open where anybody could see him – say his prayers and return to the studio to shoot the scene set up by Irani in the meantime.[36] Records and photographs show that Mehboob visited Ajmer on 23 October 1957. According to Naushad, Mehboob had made a wish at the holy shrine of Aulia Chishti there, for the film's success; but significantly, there is little representation of religious practices in Mehboob films. Any religious elements that do find representation are counterbalanced by critiques of mindless devotion, unquestioned adherence of rituals and god-dependence. It is unprofitable to look for univocal statements in a Mehboob film. Perhaps, this is why such diverse audiences have appreciated his films over so many years.

. . . .

With the film *made* and *viewed*, we can now look at the reception of *Mother India* in India and abroad. The première at the Liberty theatre, Bombay, was a grand affair; footage of it is preserved at the National Film Archive of India. Vijay Anand immortalised the event by incorporating it in his film *Kālā Bāzār* (1960), in order to illustrate the growing practice of ticket touting. Ministers, governmental officials and Reserve Bank personnel were invited, in Delhi and in respective state capitals. The shows were followed by lavish dinners; the guest list, the RSVP replies and the letters thanking the Khans for their hospitality make for interesting reading. For example, the President of India, Rajendra Prasad saw *Mother India* in the presidential quarters on 23 October, along with Prime Minister Jawaharlal Nehru and his daughter Indira Gandhi (herself Prime Minister after Nehru). Mehboob had written to the President, 'I am a film producer, who has risen in life from very humble beginnings. I have recently produced a picture called "Mother India" – a story of our soil and its children. My ambition in life is to show this picture to you at Rāshtrapati Bhavan and obtain your blessings if you like it.'

Mehboob's letter to Nehru is more intimate. 'No function in our country is complete without your dynamic personality. My prayer, therefore, is that when the President commands me to show him the picture, you should bless me with your presence and if you like the picture, oblige me with your certificate to be framed as an heirloom in my humble family.' Since Mehboob was present on that occasion, no letters exist to show what these leaders thought of the film. The director addressed Indira Gandhi as the 'mother of the nation', while requesting her to take the initiative and get her father to see the film. Gandhi conveyed the confirmation, but to Nargis instead. 'The film is drawing very good reviews. Everyone has praised your acting. The same cannot be said of the others.'

Chief Minister of West Bengal, B. C. Roy, and Governor, Padmajā Naidu, saw *Mother India* in Calcutta. Chief Minister of Mahārāshtra, Morarji Desai, opposed in principle to the medium of cinema, was apparently moved by its patriotic content and granted it exemption from entertainment tax. This meant cheaper tickets and so a larger audience – and consequently larger profits for the producers. Mehboob was eager to reap more such monetary benefit and honour. Curiously, no other state governments complied with Mehboob's requests. A thorough study of the reception of *Mother India* in individual regions of India would be of much interest, but cannot be undertaken here. The film did particularly well in Delhi, Uttar Pradesh, Gujarat, Karnātaka and Maharashtra. In the initial years, its success was resounding in Bengal (a Marxist state) and Assam. But in the south, initially only Kerala (also Marxist) had shown an overwhelming response.

The strategies Mehboob Productions adopted to promote the film over this vast land are too numerous to mention. Unbelievable but true is the practice of sending representatives to small and big cities; they carried prints to the theatres, stayed around during the three regular shows and collected the print at the end of the day. This was to ensure the film did not have unauthorised screenings (and the print was not mishandled during projection). Letters show how the Bombay office maintained close watch over these men in distant areas. Theatres were strictly forbidden to run *Mother India* at morning or matinee shows, but at the regular three slots (3, 6 and 9 p.m.) only.

According to records, there was a resurgence of interest in *Mother India* in the 1970s, with sales increasing all over the country.

There was a project to remake the film in all south Indian languages (with Raza helping the scriptwriters in the south). On 1 November 1976 Nargis attended the *mahurat* in the Prasad Studio of Madras and 'switched on the camera' for K. Vijayan's *Mother India*, in Telegu (Shivaji Ganshan and Vanishri in the lead). I had associated this revival of interest with the political state of the country at the time. Prime Minister Indira Gandhi had imposed a State of Emergency, concertedly stifling voices of dissent from opposition parties and the press. The film was aired on television, for the first time, on governmental orders. Obviously, it was perceived that the film promotes developmental activities, and discourages an individual's attempt to take the law into their own hands. Eminent painter M. F. Husain supported Indira Gandhi; he confirms he had Nargis and the film in mind when he painted a series depicting Gandhi as 'Mother India'. Shaukat Khan points out that another reason for the film's revival has to do with the improvements in sound and projection quality that most theatres introduced around this time, enabling Indian audiences to see *Mother India* in all its grandeur. Ironically, the fact that the film was in Technicolor was also the reason why many more prints could not be scored – or else, the film would have fared even better.

. . . .

Though the history of uninterrupted viewing has come to an end, the film continues to be shown periodically. In the mid-1990s, Tejaswini Apte titled a newspaper article, 'Move over *Rangeela*, *Mother India* is back and running to full houses.'[37] However, not everyone of the present generation has seen the film (or so my random survey reveals) – for some it might never have existed. During the period of my research on this book, the film had a one-week release in the Rahul theatre in Pune. The hall was empty and I wondered: 'So, this agrarian saga has finally become passé in the context of globalisation!' A week later in Bombay, travelling from the house of Naushad to the Mehboob Studios, I got talking to the young driver of the auto-rickshaw. Not only had he seen this film, he was also in a position to inform me that a recent film *Jodi No.1* (2000) cites a sequence from *Mother India* – a spoof *and* a tribute. Any simple statement about audience reception of a film like *Mother India* is bound to be inadequate and non-representative.

International distribution of the film is now practically over; but not quite. Brian Larkin writes: 'It's a Friday night in Kano, northern Nigeria and *Mother India* is playing at the Marhaba cinema. Outside, scalpers are hurriedly selling the last tickets to two thousand people lucky enough to buy seats in the open cinema in this city on the edge of Africa's Sahel desert.' He adds that most have seen the film at least fifteen times; they sing the song in Hindi and speak the actors' line on their behalf, translated into Hausa.[38] For over three decades *Mother India* established (along with Raj Kapoor's *Awāra*) the popularity of Indian films in several countries. Initially, a short international version of two hours' duration was prepared for foreign audiences. A review in the *Monthly Film Bulletin* (vol. 25, July 1958) remarked, '*Mother India* has been shortened by some 40 minutes for release in this country – and we should be grateful. Two hours of this rag-bag pantomime is enjoyable enough; more would have made this highly spiced mixture completely indigestible.' *Mother India* was dubbed in Spanish, French and Russian for foreign markets. Greece, Poland, Rumania and Czechoslovakia were first to buy the film in Europe. Its success was proverbial in Greece, Spain and Russia, where Nargis became an icon of womanhood. However, it was not a success story everywhere. Technicolor held a screening of *Mother India* for distributors and producers in Paris (around 30 June 1958). L. Goron, a producer–financer present on that occasion, wrote to Ivan Lassgallner (undated), 'Ce Mr. est le plus grand cinéaste du monde [this man is the world's greatest film-maker today].' The French version did well in the French colonies; it did some business in Paris, too. It has remained the quintessential Indian film (along with *Awāra*) for Parisians who saw the film then, titled *Les Bracelets d'or*. Goron bought a print for Brazil. Subsequently, it proved to be highly successful in Peru, Bolivia and Ecuador. In the African countries enthusiasm did not wane for decades. B. D. Garga reports, 'Well over a decade after its release in India,

Mehboob and Alexander Korda sign a contract for the distribution of *Aan*

the Cinémathèque Algérienne was showing *Mother India* to a packed house. As I watched the film, I was surprised to discover the spell a rural Indian family had cast on a wholly Arab audience.'

After some delay caused by other distributors and agents (this chapter is filled with accounts of misplaced trust and betrayal by distribution agencies and personnel), Columbia Pictures released the film in the USA and UK. An announcement in the Indian journal *Cine Advance* titled, 'American Premier of "Mother India" Today', informs the US release was on 9 July 1959.[39] The *New York Post*'s Irene Thirer reviewed the film under the title *Handful of Grain* commenting, 'We found the customs enthralling, though not at all like our own.' She praised the film's 'striking dramatic appeal' but predicted it 'might be difficult for average movie fans to appreciate completely.' *Mother India* opened at the Rialto, London, in March (previews in *Kinematograph Weekly* and *The Daily Cinema* show a further shortened version of 95 minutes was released here). It was taken to a dozen cities in England, but was far from a success. We cannot say whether poor distribution or the American audiences' inability to relate to the film accounts for the abysmal failure there. The Asian diaspora was not yet large enough to make distribution in such a large country profitable. Besides, opposed to it being shown only to the Asian population, Mehboob had forbidden screenings at or through the Asia Society. However, the American chapter becomes interesting for another reason.

In early February, the American Academy of Motion Picture Arts and Sciences asked the Film Federation of India to select a film for their 'Best Foreign Language Film' category. The president of FFI, M. B. Bilimoria, and the board members selected *Mother India*. George Seaton,

George Seaton (centre) greets Mehboob and wife before the Oscars

the Academy President cabled Mehboob on 18 February 1958, 'Pleasure to tell you India [sic] film *Mother India* has been voted nomination for Academy Foreign Film award. Other nominations are: *The Devil Came at Night*, *Gates of Paris*, *The Nights of Cabiria*, and *Nine Lines*. Congratulations.' There was an important addition, 'If you have print with English subtitles and wish to send it for final voting by Academy membership, we will be glad to receive. All other films nominated have English subtitles.' The subtitling could only be done in England; Mehboob Productions had run out of its foreign currency quota and the permission to score a fresh print was slow in coming. To make matters worse, though only five months old, the original negative had developed scratches and the Academy would not accept a flawed print. Technicolor carried out corrections using a recently developed process and the Academy passed the two sample reels. Thus, after much agony and suspense a restored and subtitled print made it to the Oscars on time. The award for the Best Foreign Language Film that year went to Fellini's *The Nights of Cabiria* (*Mother India* lost by one vote).

Mehboob Khan attended the Oscar ceremony with Sardar Akhtar and Nargis. When initially only 75 dollars was sanctioned for each of them, Mehboob sought financial assistance from Prime Minister Nehru (also the Finance Minister). 'Our picture (by "our" I mean picture belonging to our great country) has been selected as one of the five best pictures. You know I am a pure *swadeshi* [indigenous] product without any English education and I badly need the help and support of our nation's representatives in America. Like other international producers, I

A press conference after the Oscar's ceremony

should be able to show that our government is also backing me. Otherwise I will look small and lonely.' I do not know the exact details of the premier's response, but an augmented figure of 1,200 dollars each was sanctioned. India was still in transition from a feudal order to a democratic, capitalist society and it was possible to write such letters to a head of state, as if to a village elder or patriarch (Nehru was *Chacha* or Uncle to the children-of-the-nation). This letter further illuminates the behaviour of this Asian movie mogul, who could bend and be childlike before another figure of authority.

The entire experience must have been very stressful and the director suffered a heart attack on 26 March, while still in Los Angeles. After recuperating, he went to England for a vacation (and to discuss with several people a film project, to be titled *Tajmahal*, that had taken some shape in the US). He also visited Paris to discuss possible collaboration with the French inventor André Debrie to set up a colour laboratory in Bombay. The director returned to India after all this – after making 'a pilgrimage to Iraq' on the way back.

Mother India received an uncontested nomination for the Best Film of the Year, at the *Filmfare* awards (instituted by the *Times of India* group, named after their film journal of the same title). In addition, it received awards for direction (Mehboob Khan), cinematography (Faredoon Irani) and sound (Kaushik). Nargis was unanimously awarded the Best Actress. (In March 1958, the government of India bestowed on her the *Padmaśri* – for her contribution to cinema.) At the Government Film Awards (known today as the National Awards, but the State Awards, then), *Mother India* received only a Certificate of Merit as Best Feature Film in Hindi. (In December that year, Khan received an award for Best Film Publicity Material from the Advertising and Publicity Department under the Ministry of Information and Broadcasting.) There were invitations from other festivals: Karlovy Vary in Czechoslovakia (where Nargis received the 'Best Actress' award), Peru and Manila. Mehboob was invited to be a member of the jury at the Moscow International Film Festival in 1961. Meanwhile the film continued to break all box-office records throughout the country.

. . . .

Like a biography of a person, an account of a film chronicles both the time when the film was made and the time when the account is written. It tells of people and objects, other films, literature, music and the arts, numerous beliefs and practices belonging to both these periods. There are attitudes and ideological positions underlying the film, as well as the writing on it (which might or might not be explicit). The study of a film is multivalent – the plural in the term *film studies* reflects this – and so, by the time the accounting is over, it is clear that one cannot ever have the last word on a film.

In addition, films have the habit of lingering even after their circulation is practically over. For example, in the case of *Mother India*, Salman Rushdie has recently written, 'Nargis, the Indian movie star of the 1950s who later had a career in politics, once denounced the great film director Satyajit Ray for making films that offered too negative an image of India. In her own movies, she said, she had always celebrated the positive. When asked for an example, she replied, "Dams".'[40] Contiguous with the fact that many actors in India come to identify with characters who bring them recognition, and then lead their lives according to those roles, Nargis believed in the developmental progress of the country. She became involved in social work after her marriage

Mehboob receiving the state award *Padmaśri* from the President of India, S. Radhakrishnan (1963)

A party in the Mehboob Studios

Yuri Gagarin and his wife being hosted by Mehboob

and co-founded the Spastic Society of India in Bombay. In 1979, Nargis was elected an MP and denounced Ray's *Pather Panchali* in parliament, causing great controversy.[41] Many have wondered what motivated this outburst. One reason is that she apparently never forgot the *Monthly Film Bulletin* review, which also carried the following lines: 'The colourful *Mother India* makes a strong contrast with other recent Indian films seen in this country, especially those of Satyajit Ray. One admired and respected Ray's films for their almost lyrical tranquility. *Mother India* is a more typical Indian film – exotic, spectacular, and charmingly naïve, owing much to the influence of gaudiest Hollywood.'

It is very interesting that *Mother India*, designated as an epic film, is also about the Indian village and its poverty; it deals with poor peasants and not gods and kings. The kind of attention the film pays to social realities is usually associated with realism in literature and cinema – for which Ray's film has been praised. This saga of three generations of a family, exaggerated and exotic, dramatising every emotion and sentiment, dotted with songs and dances, is an example of an Indian *popular cinema* – as against Ray's film that is perceived as an *art (house) film*. If the film is maximalist (as against minimalist) in its style and treatment, so are the discussions it gives rise to.

There is something at the very end of *Mother India* that often escapes notice, but is worth further deliberation. At the end, there is no woman other than Radha – not even Ramu's wife Champa. From a film studies' point of view, it could be very satisfying that the trajectory of Radha's character is so efficiently drawn: initially an iconic figure, then an active narrative agent, an assortment of symbols, lastly a great symbol. Does it then mean Radha is a mere symbol – ultimately invisible, co-opted within a male discourse? I cannot bring any closure to this question.

From the point of view of a feminist criticism, this is how the figures of women occur in a film – as means of signification for a film's male characters and patriarchal discourse of the society. *Mother India* is no exception to this. And at the same time, such realisations are modified, when we look at the many films that have followed, inspired by it. But none generates the discussion this one does.[42] It is difficult to imagine a character like Radha in Indian cinema today. What does that mean? Surely, this is indicative of definite shifts in all the issues that were raised in this study – shifts that are commensurate with the financial, political and social changes that have been taking place. Constant reference to and comparison with the earlier film *Aurat* contributed to one set of understandings of *Mother India*. A study of later films and comparison with them,will inform us what was there but is no more, what was hoped for but is now lost. We might then arrive at an even better understanding of the phenomenon called *Mother India*.

NOTES

. . . .

1 Though the city is called 'Mumbai' now, I will use 'Bombay', in order to avoid using two different names.

2 Some junior technicians and extras received payment on a daily or shift basis. A canteen in the studio (still there) provided meals at a fair price.

3 Ardeshir Irani had also directed Iran's first sound film *The Daughter of Loristan* or *The Lur Girl* (1933) – rejuvenated today in Mohseen Makhbalbaf's brilliant *Once Upon a Time in Cinema* (1992).

4 The first evidence of Mehboob's residence is in a slum near Bombay Central. His last residence was on Bombay's plush Marine Drive, where one son, Shaukat Khan (and family), lives today with their mother Fatima.

5 The letter dated 21 May 1947 is framed and placed alongside awards and citations in Mehboob's office.

6 Mehboob was able to convince the legendary singer Begum Akhtar to act in this film. Her only other film appearance (only as a singer though) is in Ray's *Jalsāghar* (*The Music Room*, 1958).

7 Paul Willemen observes, 'The position of the family remain[s] vague, partaking of the colonially induced capitalism while simultaneously incarnating a continuation of feudal relations.' See Willemen, Paul, 'Negotiating the Transition to Capitalism: The Case of *Andaz*', in Wimal Dissanayake (ed.), *Melodrama and Asian Cinema* (Cambridge: Cambridge University Press, 1993)

8 One Safdar Nizāmi attached to the *dargāh* of Nizāmuddin Āulia in Delhi (built around the grave of the Sufi saint).

9 Emo is Eyemo, a lightweight American camera used during World War II. (Obviously, the letter is not clearly worded.)

10 Many Indians, including Gandhi and Rabindranath Tagore, had reacted strongly. Several books titled *Father India*, *Sister India*, etc. followed in its wake.

11 Mehboob dealt with Technicolor directly and not through Ramnord. However, in the credits, Mehboob acknowledges Ramnord, the agent for Technicolor in India.

12 Mehta is celebrated for his cinematography in films like *Hum Dil De Chuke Sanam* (1999) and *Lagaan* (2001).

13 Indian directors like Mehboob Khan and Raj Kapoor often used the axis-jump for various ends.

14 Nargis and Kapoor were among the first to become life members of the WICA. *The First 25 Years, Indian Cinematography*, Western India Cinematographers' Association, 1993.

15 Nargis, in 'The Postman Knocks at Ivory Tower', *Filmfare*, 3 January, 1958.

16 A quasi-magic, quasi-anthropomorphic design found in rock paintings, seals and pottery – from Mohenjodaro in the west to Udaygiri in the east, and in all later strata of civilisation. Eventually, it came to be associated with Śrī or Lakshmi.

17 Traditionally, ornaments are meant to be a woman's personal property. As Radha takes them off, she is placing them at the service of her new family.

18 The Sanskrit word for salt, *lavan*, also means beauty and grace. *Lāvanya*, used today in the sense of a woman's charm only, earlier also meant 'saltiness'.

19 *Deewar* (1975) has been seen as the most important example of this trend.

20 Sajid was sent to St Peter's School in Panchgani (where Mehboob's sons had studied). Mehboob conceived his next film *Son of India* (1962) exclusively for Sajid; the film was a failure.

21 The story of Krishna begins with several patriarchal figures: his father, imprisoned by another king (his mother's brother) and his adoptive father, a pastoral chieftain. Krishna stealing cream and butter from the adoptive father's larder and distributing them to poor peasant boys has been seen as a benevolent as well as a political act. The antecedents to Krishna are local hero figures coming to the rescue of the oppressed, during constant flux in the political state in innumerable fiefdoms. They would become local deities and gradually be identified with Krishna – consolidating Krishna worship.

22 In another milestone *Sholay* (1975), a character would have his arms cut off by the villain; he would *remain* on the scene and take revenge.

23 At times, she is shorn of all ornaments, seated head hung in dejection; at times a resplendent queen mother accompanied by her *children* – common people or leading statesmen. *Ānandamath* (1952), a film in Hindi, was made by Hemen Gupta, whose films were almost all banned during British rule.

24 Set to music by Rabindranath Tagore, it was sung at the National Congress meeting in 1911. Its status has been equal to the official anthem by Tagore: one would inaugurate and the latter close a public function.

25 Gandhi's reply to Mayo states he would prefer it if some others occupied India rather than 'this slow emasculation at the hands of the British'.

26 This phrase is from *Suvarnarekhā* (1964) by Ritwik Ghatak.

27 *Atharva Veda*, book 12, verses 5–12 in particular.

28 Films like *Dharti Ke Lal* (1946) and *Chinnamul* (1950), used documentary footage of the Bengal famine of 1942 and the mass exodus in its wake.

29 The motif of an ignorant man going to a woman with a desire for learning features in many films, e.g. from *Sri 420* (1955) to a blockbuster *Maine Pyar Kiya* (1989).

30 Mehboob Studios had projection facilities and many guests saw Mehboob's films there.

31 The filled water pot, necessary for all religious and social functions, represents the human womb and cosmic origin of things.

32 In particular the Nāth sect – extremely popular but at the same time marginalised by mainstream Brahmanic religion. Interestingly, the first line of the song occurs in many actual Nāth compositions.

33 Many people I spoke to quoted this (in many different versions). However, this sentiment

definitely hides within it sexist and ageist sentiments; for implicit in it is the fact that only parents can hurt children or men their women.

34 *Muddai lākh burā cāhe to kyā hotā hai? Wohi hotā hai jo manẓur-é khudā hotā hai.*

35 Krishna would gradually lose this position and the representation of Ram would become, from the late 1980s onwards, principal icon for a resurgence of militant nationalism.

36 A similar account comes from Peter Pitt, sound editor for *Aan*, cited by Munni Kabir.

37 *The Asian Age*, 15 November 1995. Apte elaborates on the film's problematic relationship with nationalism. (*Rangūla* is a box-office hit and something of a cult film.)

38 'Bollywood Comes to Nigeria' in www.samarmagazine.org/archive/bollywoodnigeria

39 The *Variety* review shows the film was shown with an Indian title, *Bharat-mata*.

40 *Big Dams, Contempt of Court and the Narmada Movement* (circulated by www.sarai.net).

41 Sunil Dutt too became an MP and stood for election several times representing the Congress party. His campaign poster (1985) carried the slogan 'Mother India needs you'.

42 The list is long: *Gangā-Jumnā* (1961), *Deewar* (1975), *Rām-Lakhan* (1989), etc. *Godmother* (1989), about a woman's rise as an underworld don, is a recent and important example; the director of this film, Vinay Shukla, has written extensively about how he was inspired by *Mother India*. Two south Indian films titled *Mother India* were made in 1992 and 1995, but these were not remakes of Mehboob's film.

CREDITS

· ·

Mother India

India
1957

Production Company
Mehboob Productions
Producer
Mehboob Khan
Chief Production Executive
V. J.Shah
Production Manager
M. A. Qureshi
Director
Mehboob
Assistant Directors
Chimankant Gandhi, S. A. Master, Ahmad Hussain, Nazar Ahmed, Ahmed G. Seikh, Syed Ameeruddin, Wajid Hussain
Dialogue
Vajahat Mirza, S. Ali Raza
Songs/Lyrics
Shakeel Badayuni
Music
Naushad
Music Assistant
Mohomed Ebrahim
Cinematography
Faredoon Irani
Assistant Cameramen
Balu T. Sawant, M. R. Vasudev, Parvez Savawala
Sound
Kaushik
Sound Assistant
P. P. Boloor, M. A. Sheikh, Manohar
Editing
Shamsuddin Kadri
Editing Assistant
A. H. Ratia, I. Baporia
Art Direction
V. H. Palnitkar
Settings
D. R. Jadav, Munawar Ali Mistri

Settings Assistant
Y. H. Bargal
Dance Direction
Chiman Seth
Dances
Mazgaon Mitra Mandal, Sanskar Stri Mandal, Sorthi Ghedia Gnati Garbi Mandal
Costumes
Fazaldin
Costume Assistant
Alla Ditta, Amarnath
Make-up
P. G. Joshi
Make-up Assistant
R. Pitambar
Chief Electrician
M. B. Ansari
Publicity
Nanubhai N. Shukla
Stills
Gunavant Patel

Cast
Radha
Nargis
Birju
Sunil Dutt
Ramu
Rajendra Kumar
Shyamu
Raaj Kumar
Sukhi-lala
Kanhaiyalal
Sundar-chachi
Jiloo Maa
Shambhu
Muqri
Ramu, when a child
Master Surendra
Birju, when a child
Master Sajid
Radha's third son
Master Alec
Champa
Kumkum **Birju, when a Rupa**
Chanchal

Chandra
Azra
Kamala
Sheela Nayak
The Schoolteacher, Lalita Prasad
Siddiqui
Sukhi-lala's goons (described as his 'A.D.C.')
Ram Shastri, Faquir Mohamed, Jwala Singh
Village girls
Geeta, Hameeda

Colour
15,642 feet
(length at the time of Censor)
Gevacolor negatives Processed at Film Centre Bombay under the supervision of Messrs. Vender Awera and W. Seys Technicolor prints: Technicolor Ltd., London, through Messrs. Ramnord Research Laboratories Ltd., Bombay
Recorded on RCA sound system
Gramophone Records on HMV

Censor Certificate
7 July 1957

Release in India begins 25 October 1957 with
The Bombay circuit: Mehboob Pictures
Bengal: Hindustan Super Films Pvt Ltd
Delhi and U.P.: Indra Films Tamilnadu: Narayan & Co. Rajasthan: Eveready Pictures, Indore

The Central Provinces:
Kalyan Pictures, Amaravati
East Punjab: The All India
Film Corp. Ltd., Jullunder
City
Andhra Pradesh: Navayug
Films, Vijaywada

Nizam's Estate: Select
Pictures, Secundrabad

USA release
Columbia, 9 July 1959

British release
Columbia, 1961

South East Asia
Shaw Bros. Singapore

Overseas territories
Overseas Film Corporation,
Bombay/Wentways
Productions Ltd

BIBLIOGRAPHY

Anderson, Benedict, *Imagined Communities:
Reflections of the Origin and Spread of
Nationalism* (London: Verso, 1983)

Butler, Judith, *The Psychic Life of Power: Theories
in Subjection* (California: Stanford University
Press, 1997)

Chakravarty, Dipesh, *Provincializing Europe:
Postcolonial Thought and Historical Difference*
(Princeton, NJ: Princeton University Press, 2000)

Chakravarty, Sumita S., *National Identity in Indian
Popular Cinema 1947–1987* (Austin: University of
Texas Press, 1993)

Chatterjee, Gayatri, *Awāra* (New Delhi: Wiley
Eastern, 1992)

Chatterjee, Partho, *The Nation and Its Fragments*
(Princeton, NJ: Princeton University Press, 1993)

Gell, Alfred, *Art and Agency: An Anthropological
Theory* (Oxford: Clarendon Press, 1998)

George, T. G. S., *The Life and Times of Nargis*
(New Delhi: HarperCollins, 1994)

Hardiman, David, *Feeding the Baniya: Peasants
and Usurers in Western India* (New Delhi:
Oxford University Press, 1996)

Inden, Ronald, *Imagining India* (London: Basil
Blackwell, 1990)

Kabir, Nasreen Munni, *Bollywood, The Indian
Cinema Story* (London: Channel 4 Books/
Macmillan, 2001)

Kaplan, E. Ann, *Motherhood and Representation:
The Mother in Popular Culture and Melodrama*
(London: Routledge, 1992)

Rajadhyaksha, Ashish and Paul Willemen,
Encyclopaedia of Indian Cinema (New Delhi:
Oxford University Press, 1997)

Singer, Milton (ed.), *Krishna: Myths, Rites and
Attitudes* (Honolulu: East-West Centre Press, 1966)

Sivaramamurti, C., *Lakshmi in Indian Art and
Thought* (New Delhi: Kanak, 1982)

Stoler Miller, Barbara, *Gita Govinda of Jayadev:
Love Song of the Dark Lord* (New York:
Columbia University Press, 1977)

Taussig, Michael, *Mimesis and Alterity* (London
and New York: Routledge, 1993)

Whitney, William Dwight Whitney tr., *Atharva
Veda Samhita* (Delhi: Motilal Banarasidass,
Indian reprint, 1962)

ARTICLES AND REVIEWS

Apte, Tejaswini, 'Move Over *Rangeela, Mother
India* is Back and Running', *The Asian Age*,
15 November 1995

Baghdadi, Rafiq and Rajiv Rao, 'Mehboob Khan:
A Director by Default, Not Choice', *The Asian
Age*, 19 May 1994

Bhattacharya, Roshmila, '*Mother India*, Terms of
Endurance', *Screen*, 18 May 2001

Biswas, Moinak, *Narrating the Nation: Mother
India and Roja*, unpublished article held by the
author and the National Film Archive of India

Garga, B. D., 'The Feel of the Good Earth',
Cinema In India, vol. 3 no.2, April/June 1989

Geetha J., 'The Mutating Mother: From *Mother
India* to *Ram Lakhan*', *Deep Focus*, vol. 3 no. 3,
1990

Hariharan, K., 'Revisiting *Mother India*', *Sound,
Light, Action*, vol. 2, 2000

Patel, Baburao, '"Mother India" Becomes The
Pride Of India', *Film India*, December 1957.

Rangoonwalla, Firoze, 'Mehboob created popular
hits and films ahead of his time', *Screen*, vol. 33
no. 3, November 1992

Sathe, V. P., 'The Making of *Mother India*', *The
Movie*, July 1984

Thomas, Rosie, 'Sanctity and Scandal: The
Mythologization of Mother India', *Quarterly
Review of Film and Video*, vol. 2 no. 3, 1989

ALSO PUBLISHED

If you would like further information about future BFI Film Classics or about other books from BFI Publishing, please sign up to our mailing list at www.palgrave.com/bfi.

You can also write to:
BFI/Palgrave Macmillan Ltd
Houndmills
Basingstoke
RG21 6XS UK